How to Write a
KILLER LinkedIn® Profile
. . . and 18 Mistakes to Avoid

by Brenda Bernstein, The Essay Expert

If you **follow the advice** in this book, you will attract more readers, and the ones you attract will read more of what you have to say. You will build trust and impress your target market. That means you have the best possible chance of getting the RESULTS that you want. That's why you have a profile on LinkedIn in the first place, right? Why would you take a chance by doing anything else?

— **Brenda Bernstein**,
TheEssayExpert.com

APPRECIATIONS

Every writer needs an editor, and I have benefited from multiple eagle eyes as this book has taken shape! From dear friends and family to loyal e-book readers and my virtual assistant Jeanne Goodman, a formidable group has formed a team behind me. Typos happen, but there are fewer in these pages than there would have been without the keen eyes of many generous souls! Special thanks goes to my e-book publisher, Brian Schwartz, as well as to Robin Krauss, who tackled the monumental task of converting an e-book to print!

Each person who has written a recommendation for me on LinkedIn has made my Top-Ranked status in the Amazon Business Writing category a possibility. Each person who has chosen to be part of my affiliate program makes this important information available to a wider audience. And my public relations man, Scott Becher, has been relentless in connecting me with media opportunities.

Thank you to all of you, and to many more I did not mention, for making *How to Write a KILLER LinkedIn Profile* a success!

And thank you in advance for your generosity in considering reviewing this book on Amazon. Your support makes a difference.

Post a review on Amazon!

How to Write a KILLER LinkedIn Profile... And 18 Mistakes to Avoid: 2015 Edition (11th Edition) May 29, 2014
by Brenda Bernstein

Kindle Edition
$9.97
Auto-delivered wirelessly

⭐⭐⭐⭐½ ▾ 278

Books: See all 26 items

Customer Reviews

⭐⭐⭐⭐½ 278
4.7 out of 5 stars ▾

5 star		78%
4 star		14%
3 star		4%
2 star		2%
1 star		2%

Share your thoughts with other customers

See all 278 customer reviews ›

TABLE OF CONTENTS

Appendices

REVIEWS

Having inserted relevant keywords into my LinkedIn profile, I reached top position for my area of expertise and location. And this has helped me receive several offers from headhunters and CEOs searching LinkedIn for people with my profile. Just this month, I started a new job—and guess what? The CEO of my new company contacted me through LinkedIn. Thanks, Brenda!

— **Charlotte L.**, Editor,
Barcelona, Spain

Thanks to Brenda's common-sense, actionable steps, I easily raised my LinkedIn profile to "All-Star" status. Read this book, follow Brenda's advice, and watch your LinkedIn network take off!

— **Christopher Kruchten**, Marketing Customer Service Supervisor,
Madison, WI

I saw a sustained 4-5X traffic increase on LinkedIn in by the time I was done. [My new profile] led to many new business contacts as well as an invite for an advisory board seat at a top university.

— **Joseph P.**, Board of Advisors at NJIT,
New York, NY

To say this book is a 'Must Have' is like saying you should have a Bible.

— **J. R. Hollingsworth**, JD, Director of the Job Seekers Network

As a resume and LinkedIn profile writer, I found Brenda's book to be one of the best out there.

— **Lynn Levy**, Career Coach & Resume Writer,
Boston, MA

I have been contacted by numerous recruiters, and it has only been four days since I purchased the book! Now, I have people at work asking me to help them work on their accounts. MUST buy!!!

— **Bill Cozad**, Account Manager,
Milwaukee, WI

My LinkedIn rating went from 17% to 95%. I have received calls from recruiters who called after looking at my revised profile. This is a very worthwhile investment—can't recommend it enough!

— **Simon A.**, Writer, Production Manager,
Vancouver, Canada

I already got a job interview! I am at the top of the search function list for my industry in a 50-mile radius, so I am very happy. This book is very easy to use and the tips are a great help.

— **Matthew W.**, EMT,
Orange County, CA

Brenda promises that "your numbers will soar if you follow the advice given" (and I would agree). This . . . fun and quick read . . . will provide insights to even the most experienced LinkedIn users.

— **Thomas M. Loarie**, Amazon Top 1000 Reviewer,
Danville, CA

I consider myself tech savvy and I didn't think that there was much Brenda could teach me about LinkedIn. I was wrong.

— **Zachary Fichman-Klein**, Industrial Skills Trainer,
Saudi Arabia

Best ROI ever!!!

— **Marco Flaccavento**, CAIA level II candidate, CFA level II candidate,
United Kingdom

I have had a 73% increase in profile views in the last week. Thank You!

— **Simon Crowther**, Project Manager,
Greater Manchester, UK

As a LinkedIn trainer myself, it's good to know I have a resource like this for my clients to help them after they've left my classroom.

— **Michael Phelps**, LinkedIn Trainer,
Little Rock, AR

I am located in a small country in Europe but the results are as promised. Brenda has hit the nail on the head. If you are serious about your career and social media in the workplace, you need to get this book.

— **Jan A. Jensen**, Owner, Z-Solutions, Ltd,
Zurich, Sweden

ABOUT THE AUTHOR

| Certified Master Resume Writer | Certified Advanced Resume Writer | Certified Executive Resume Writer | 2013 Best International Resume 2nd Place Winner | 2013 Best Sales Resume Nominee | 2012 Best New Graduate Resume 3rd Place Winner | 2012 Best Re-Entry Resume Nominee | 2011 Best Creative Resume Nominee |

Brenda Bernstein, Founder and Senior Editor at The Essay Expert LLC, is a #1 best-selling author, an in-demand speaker & consultant, and an award-winning resume writer holding Certified Executive Resume Master and Certified Master Resume Writer certifications from Career Directors International. *How to Write a KILLER LinkedIn Profile*, her very first book, has been featured in Fortune and Forbes Magazines; the book has commanded the top ranking in Amazon's business writing skills e-book category since July 2012. Her other e-books, *How to Write a WINNING Resume . . . 50 Tips to Reach Your Job Search Target*[1] and *How to Write a STELLAR Executive Resume . . . 50 Tips to Reach Your Job Search Target*[2], have been met with rave reviews

A top-notch editor, Brenda has over 15 years of successful written communications experience from C- level executive resume development to business copy editing to Ivy-League-bound student college essay consulting.

She holds a B.A. in English from Yale University and a J.D. from the New York University School of Law, graduating from both schools with honors. Brenda's clients report that they gain clarity about themselves and their message, in addition to having that message deliver sought-after results.

- Email: BrendaB@TheEssayExpert.com
- Web: TheEssayExpert.com
- LinkedIn: LinkedIn.com/in/brendabernstein
- Facebook: Facebook.com/TheEssayExpert
- Phone: 608-467-0067

---

1 How to Write a WINNING Resume . . . 50 Tips to Reach Your Job Search Target
http://www.amazon.com/gp/product/B00F05WFX0/

2 How to Write a STELLAR Executive Resume . . . 50 Tips to Reach Your Job Search Target
http://www.amazon.com/gp/product/B00F05W9I6/

INTRODUCTION

Why Should You Read this Book?

LinkedIn hosts the profiles of more than 380 million people in over 200 countries and it is the 3rd fastest growing social network. In a July 2013 *Fortune* Magazine article entitled, LinkedIn: How It's Changing Business (And How to Make it Work for You)[1], journalist Jessi Hempel asserts, "In the past year LinkedIn has emerged as one of the most powerful business tools on the planet." The current numbers reported by LinkedIn are 97 million monthly visitors worldwide, 50% of which are logging on via mobile devices. Furthermore, 88 of the *Fortune* 100 use LinkedIn's licensed recruiting software to search for job candidates.

Numerous studies, by entities including Microsoft, Reppler, Jobvite and Bullhorn, show convincingly that more than 75% of employers actively research candidates online—and that 97.3% of staffing professionals overall use LinkedIn as a recruiting tool.[2] They show further that approximately 70% have decided NOT to hire a candidate based on what they've found—and that a similar percentage have hired employees based on the person's online presence. Here's the clincher: A whopping 89% of all recruiters report having hired someone through LinkedIn (as opposed to 26% from Facebook and 15% from Twitter).

LinkedIn has even expanded its customer base to high school students, lowering the minimum age for membership in the U.S. to 14 and creating LinkedIn University Pages[3] where students can get information about and engage in discussions with universities worldwide. If you are a high school student, now is the time to start building your network and exploring career opporties! (See High School Students: Embrace your skills, show your professional side, and create a LinkedIn Profile.[4]) Join the over 39 million students and recent college graduates who have already taken the leap (also see Appendix J).

What's crystal clear is that every single EMPLOYER or CLIENT who considers hiring you will Google you, click on your LinkedIn profile, and assess it. Studies report that half of all LinkedIn users spend almost two hours per week using the platform, and that number is rising. Whether you are a high school or college student, job seeker, company owner or other professional, your profile MUST impress your audience if you want results from this social media treasure chest.**

Quoted from the article The Most Important LinkedIn Page You've Never Seen[5] by WIRED author Alexandra Chang:

"Nathanson [of Rapid7] finds the vast majority of future employees on LinkedIn. And if you aren't on LinkedIn?

---

1 LinkedIn: How It's Changing Business (And How to Make it Work for You) - http://tinyurl.com/m6yt6k2

2 New Survey: LinkedIn More Dominant Than Ever Among Job Seekers And Recruiters, But Facebook Poised To Gain http://tinyurl.com/az9hpp3

3 Introducing LinkedIn University Pages - http://tinyurl.com/az9hpp3

4 High School Students: Embrace your skills, show your professional side, and create a LinkedIn Profile - http://tinyurl.com/lx78efl

5 The Most Important LinkedIn Page You've Never Seen http://www.wired.com/2013/04/the-real-reason-you-should-care-about-linkedin/

He'll probably never find you. And even if he did, he probably wouldn't hire you. 'I'm always amazed at people who aren't there now,' Nathanson says. 'When I talk to candidates and they aren't on there that's a big red flag for me.'"

Are you getting the results that you want from your LinkedIn profile?

If not, this book is for you. I provide you with 18 detailed strategies and writing tips that will teach you how to get found on LinkedIn, and how to keep people reading after they find you.

Using LinkedIn to its full potential can lead you to results you never imagined. Many of my clients have been amazed to get hired solely on the strength of their LinkedIn profile activity and content. I personally have built my business through the connections I've made on LinkedIn. If you want to read more success stories, read the LinkedIn Official Blog[6] and check out stories like account manager Sabrina Lee's at Finding My Way Home on LinkedIn[7] and digital marketer Mei Lee's at My Secret Career Weapon: LinkedIn.[8]

Over the past several years, I have worked with social media experts, business people, recruiters and employers and have identified EIGHTEEN common weak points in LinkedIn profile strategy and content. These errors can be fatal if you want people not just to find your profile, but to continue reading once they do. By following the advice below, you will avoid these errors and create a frequently visited AND highly effective LinkedIn profile.

Use these tips to create a POWERFUL profile – and show your target audience you're serious about your online presence. What's the reward? That depends on what you're looking for:

A new job . . . An unexpected partnership . . . A lucrative account . . .

YOU get to choose.

> **Important Note #1:** Some industries and companies have strict legal or corporate guidelines about what you can include in your LinkedIn profile. Nothing in this book is meant to contradict those guidelines. Please consult with your company and/or an attorney before making changes to your profile that might conflict with company policy or the legalities of your profession.

> **Important Note #2:** LinkedIn changes its platform frequently. In an interview with SocialTimes, Amy Parnell, Director of User Experience at LinkedIn said, "We are in a constant state of evolution with our site and app designs, and strive to push the experience and product value to new heights on an ongoing basis."[9]

---

6 LinkedIn® Official Blog - http://blog.linkedin.com/

7 Finding My Way Home on LinkedIn - http://blog.linkedin.com/2014/04/09/finding-my-way-home-on-linkedin/

8 My Secret Career Weapon: LinkedIn - http://blog.linkedin.com/2014/03/04/my-secret-career-weapon-linkedin/

9 SocialTimes - http://tinyurl.com/nwbdjvx

I do my best to keep up with these changes and release new editions regularly. If you discover any outdated information in this book, rest assured that an update is on its way! Check out the **Important Opportunities to Give and Receive** section of this book to read how you can get free new editions of *How to Write a KILLER LinkedIn Profile* in PDF format for a lifetime!

Important Note #3: The advice in this book works no matter what country you live in. However, the tone of the samples is geared toward the United States job market. In some countries, a subtler tone might be warranted.

LinkedIn® Profile Nuts and Bolts

This section covers some fairly straightforward "nuts and bolts" for the top portion of your profile, including your headline, photo, websites, and public profile URL. Most of the tips in this section hold keys to being found on LinkedIn. You must have keywords that people are searching for, and you must have them in the right places. You must have a robust network of at least 500 people. You must have a photo that engages your readers. And you must have a 100% complete profile, or something very close to 100%!

Completing the organizations, job titles, degrees, and dates in your Experience and Education sections is also essential to having a respectable profile, but since I have not seen many profiles that don't have this information filled in, I don't address it specifically in this section.

You may want to address the items in this section before moving on and getting creative with your Summary and Experience sections. However, some people like to wait until they have a KILLER LinkedIn Profile before they start sharing it with the world, so you might opt to complete your entire profile, including your Summary, Experience and more, before building your network. It's up to you!

MISTAKE #1

Selling Yourself Short: Lack of Keywords and an Ineffective Headline

"Keywords" are the words and phrases in your profile that match the terms web users type into their search boxes when conducting searches. For example, if you include the keywords "Sports Writer" in your LinkedIn profile, then when someone searches LinkedIn for a "Sports Writer" you will come up in the search. Here's the screen you'll see when you click the Advanced button on LinkedIn:

The more often a particular word or phrase shows up in your profile, the more likely it is that you will appear in people's searches when they look for that word or phrase.

One of the most important places to put keywords is in your headline. The "headline" on LinkedIn is the line under your name, and it is one of the first things people see when they look at your profile.

It might not be obvious that your zip code is a type of keyword in a way, especially if you are a job seeker. Recruiters look for job seekers by location! You will be asked to enter your zip code when you first create your account, and you must do so carefully.

The Problem

There are more than 300 million professionals using LinkedIn, 100 million of whom are in the United States; and the site is growing exponentially with more than two new members joining every second (check out Wikipedia[1] and the infographic from LinkedIn[2] in Appendix M). How will you possibly be found amongst all these people if you don't optimize your keywords? The answer is: You probably won't.

In your headline, for instance, brief titles such as "IT Consultant," "Sports Executive" or "Sales Professional" don't distinguish you from every other person with the same title in a pool of almost 300 million LinkedIn profiles. You must distinguish yourself in your headline to stand out, with both keywords and an attention-getting statement. Otherwise you won't get to the top of LinkedIn search results and you won't capture your readers' attention.

If you use a zip code for a remote area of the country and you're looking for a job in a major city, you will not appear in recruiter searches. Recruiters have the ability to search for potential candidates within a range of miles from any zip code. You want to be appear in those searches!

The Tune-Up

Put yourself in the position of the people who are searching for you, whether they be clients, recruiters or other partners, and identify the phrases they would be searching for. These keywords might include job titles, core competencies, geographical regions, technical skills, soft skills, languages and more.

If you are a job seeker, look at job advertisements for your target position and count keywords that are showing up repeatedly; if you like cool online tools, put the copy from a few listings into Wordle.net and create a word map that shows you what words come up most frequently. Use those keywords! And—important—use a zip code that is close to the area where you want to work! If you are able to work in Chicago but live 25 miles away in the suburbs, for instance, use a zip code half-way between that will capture searches looking for someone within a 10-mile radius of either downtown Chicago or your suburb.

Getting back to keywords: You know your profession better than anyone, so simply brainstorming commonly used words in your field can reap the perfect keywords. Another great tactic is looking at profiles of other people with similar backgrounds or positions to yours. You can also use the Skills section and scan through the dropdown menus there to see what keywords LinkedIn suggests for your profession. For more about adding skills, see Mistake #11.

Once you have identified your top keywords, add as many of them as possible in the following sections: **Headline, Current Job Title, Summary, Specialties** (if you have this section), **Additional Job Titles, and Interests.** The Advanced Search tool searches entire profiles, so insert your keywords throughout! Use them early (at the beginning of your profile) and often, while keeping your language natural (i.e., don't overload to the point of offense just for the sake of keyword optimization). Before I tell my own story and suggest best practices for headlines, allow me to provide an example of what not to do. Here it is:

---

1 Wikipedia on LinkedIn - http://en.wikipedia.org/wiki/LinkedIn

2 **300 Million Members Infographic** - http://www.slideshare.net/linkedin/300-million-linkedin-members

Interests

Living a good life. HR, HR, HR, HR, HR, HR, HR, HR, HR, HR, HR, HR, HR, HR, HR, HR, HR, HR, HR, HR, HR, HR, HR, HR, HR, HR, Talent Acquisition, Talent Manager, Nurse Recruiter, Allied Health Recruiter, Recruiter, Recruiter, Recruiter, Recruiter, Recruiter, Recruiter, Recruiter, Talent Management, Talent Management, Talent Management, Talent Acquisition, Talent Acquisition, Talent Acquisition, Sourcer, Sourcer, Sourcing, Sourcing, Recruiter, Recruiter, Recruiter, Recruiter, Recruiter, Recruiting, Recruiting, Talent Management, Talent Management, Talent Management, Talent Acquisition, Talent Acquisition, Talent Acquisition, Sourcer, Sourcer, Sourcer, Sourcer, Sourcer, Sourcer, Recruiter, Recruiter, Recruiter, Recruiter, Employee Relations Manager, Employee Relations Manager, Employee Relations Manager, Employee Relations Manager, Employee Relations Manager, Employee Relations Manager, Employee Relations Manager, Employee Relations Manager, Employee Relations Manager

Although you might be found in a search because of this keyword-packed profile, the average reader will get turned off immediately.

Use keywords, and use them wisely.

Before I knew the power of keywords, my headline read: **Founder and Senior Editor, The Essay Expert.** Note the lack of keywords in that headline! Now it reads:

Brenda Bernstein

Resume & LinkedIn Profile Writer, Author, Speaker ★
Executive Resumes ★ Executive LinkedIn Profiles ★
College Essays

Madison, Wisconsin Area | Writing and Editing

The new headline has a lot more keywords. When I changed my headline, as well as added more keywords to my Current Job Title, Summary, Specialties and other Job Titles, I went from being almost invisible in searches to coming up first in the search rankings on queries for "Executive Resume Writer" in my geographic area of Madison, WI.

Craft a headline for your profile that tells us what makes you unique and that includes as many keywords as possible. Here are some examples:

Frank Kanu 1st

Management / Business Consultant ■ Speaker ■ Author
■ Leading Fortune 500 and Small Business Executives &
Teams

Jacksonville, Florida Area | Management Consulting

Michelle Henry 1st

Executive well-versed in Strategic Planning, Capacity
Building, Program Implementation & Partnership
Development

Greater New York City Area | Nonprofit Organization Management

Nilesh Patel 1st

Experienced in Human Resources & Employment Law,
Career Counseling, and Nonprofit Management.

Greater New York City Area | Nonprofit Organization Management

See the advantage over headlines like "Consultant," "Senior VP" or "Project Manager"? More explicit headlines give spark and color to your profile as opposed to just listing your job title; and they contain keywords to help you appear at the top of search results. They can also hint at your personality, the results you produce, and some of your "soft skills."

> **NOTE:** Including proper keywords does not guarantee your profile will appear at the top of searches. There are other factors that go into search rankings, most notably your number of connections and your percent profile completeness. But without keywords, your profile is guaranteed to remain at the bottom of the pile.

What if I've never held the position I want to be found for?

If you are seeking a position as VP of Finance, and you have never held that position before, consider creative ways of including the keywords VP and Finance. For example: VP-Level Finance Executive or Available for VP of Finance Position at Growing Company.

Of course you need to make sure not to misrepresent yourself, so you might need to say "Poised for . . . " or something similar. Note that if you have performed the functions to match a job title, you can put the job title in your headline. I say if you've done the job, you can claim the job title!

Should I include a tagline?

Greig Wells of BeFoundJobs has done research that proves you will have a higher conversion rate if you include a tagline or "unique selling proposition" in addition to straight keywords in your headline. Best strategy: Use keywords to increase the frequency with which you are found in searches; include a tagline or USP to generate interest so people click to read more.

Once you have decided on your most effective Headline strategy, here's how to add it to your profile — and some pitfalls to avoid:

Click on your highlighted headline.

Brenda Bernstein ✎

Resume & LinkedIn Profile Writer, Author, Speaker ★
Executive Resumes ★ Executive LinkedIn Profiles ★
College Essays

Madison, Wisconsin Area | Writing and Editing ✎

Current	The Essay Expert, Kaplan, Inc. ✎
Previous	University of Wisconsin Law School - Career Services, CAMBA Legal Services, CAMBA Tenant Support Services
Education	New York University School of Law ✎

View profile as ▼   **500+** connections

https://www.linkedin.com/in/brendabernstein   Contact Info

You will then have an opportunity to edit "Your professional headline."

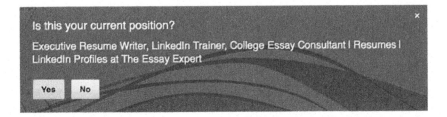

BE CAREFUL IF YOU CHANGE YOUR CURRENT POSITION!

Whenever you add a current position on LinkedIn, the program will automatically replace your headline with the current position. Make sure you save the headline you want so that you can quickly replace it. Similarly, if your headline and current job title don't match, LinkedIn will prompt you frequently with a box that looks like this:

If you click Yes, your headline will be replaced. Click No to avoid having to create your custom headline all over again.

How Do I Include Keywords in My Job Titles?

The job title fields are extremely important places to include keywords. Don't forget them! Don't feel stuck in having to put just your official job title in the job title field. You have 100 characters to play with, so use them! Here are some examples of job titles that are keyword optimized:

EXAMPLE #1: **Senior Legal Manager / Counsel**

Senior Legal Manager - EMEA I Trusted Legal Counsel I International Deals I Compliance Regional Senior Legal Counsel Middle East I Contract Management I Due Diligence I Project Execution

EXAMPLE #2: **Technology Sales Executive**

Sales & Channel Account Manager, Major Accounts I Enterprise Technology I Channel Strategy Business Development / Sales Manager I Cloud Computing I Technology Storage Sales Executive I Technology Solutions I OEM Business / Sales Development Manager I SaaS Technology I Channel Sales Channel Sales Executive I Technology I OEM

Results to Expect

You can see the results for yourself. Enter your keywords and do an "Advanced" search on LinkedIn. How close to the top of the results list are you? Keep working with your keywords until you move as high as you can in the rankings.

> **Note:** You need to have as many connections as possible to have the best chance of showing up on people's searches **(See Mistake #6)**.

More keywords in your headline means you will rank higher in searches – *more people will find you.* And with an effective tagline, people will be sufficiently intrigued to read more. An increase in page views means more potential business for you. Keywords are your key to success.

Research indicates that a strong LinkedIn presence will help you appear in Google searches as well. According to BrandYourself, LinkedIn is the social network that most often appears at the top of Google search results, ranking "higher than all other profiles including all other social networks and website builders."[3]

> **Special Note:** Some people have attempted to "stuff" keywords in their profile by adding them to their Name Field. This strategy is against LinkedIn's Terms of Service! If you have questions about what you can and can't include in the Name Field, see LinkedIn's Help Center articles, Your Profile Name and Adding a Suffix or Certifications to Your Profile Name.

> **Option:** If you need professional assistance with crafting your Headline, contact The Essay Expert. All of our LinkedIn Summary packages[4] include a custom headline that will help you move up in LinkedIn search rankings.

---

3 Here's How to Appear Higher on Google Search Results Infograhic - http://mashable.com/2012/08/02/higher-google-search-results/

4 The Essay Expert's LinkedIn Summary packages - http://theessayexpert.com/services-rates/linkedin-profiles/

MISTAKE #2

Unprofessional/Distracting Profile Photo, No Photo, or No Background Image

The Problem

Having no LinkedIn profile photo means your profile is not 100% complete. It also leaves your audience with only words to go on, and your profile will likely be skipped in favor of those with professional photos. Think about it: If you were to look at two profiles side by side, and both people had the same qualifications, and the only difference was that one person had a photo and the other did not, which one would you look at first? You might even wonder whether the person without a photo could be a spammer (there are plenty of those on LinkedIn).

Photos are particularly important for job seekers, since recruiters report they like to see photos in profiles. A study by The Ladders[1] revealed that when recruiters review your profile, they spend one fifth of that time looking at your photo! If your photo includes your dog, cat, husband, or a lot of unnecessary objects in the background, viewers might think you're immature or unprofessional, or simply be distracted; and it will be hard to focus on YOU. If you are not looking at the camera, people might not be inclined to trust you as a capable business person.

Also, if you haven't changed your profile photo since LinkedIn increased the standard profile image size, your photo may be too small for the designated area and can look unprofessional. Here's an example:

Similarly, if you have a LinkedIn Premium account, having no background image leaves your profile lacking the simple magnetic power a stunning photo could add. Here's what the standard boring blue background looks like:

---

1 Keeping an Eye on Recruiter Behavior - http://tinyurl.com/cb9m8yn

The Tune-Up

PHOTOS

Get a professional head shot with a plain background. If possible, find someone who does "branded photography" which is a way you can ensure your personality comes through your photo. If a professional photo is not an option, stand outside on a bright day, in an open space, and get a friend to take a close-up. Use natural light (not a flash which can create shadows). Smile and look directly at the camera. Make sure you portray yourself as you want to be seen by your intended audience.

If your photo is too small for the new image size, update it!

LINKEDIN'S OFFICIAL PHOTO GUIDELINES:

- Format should be jpg, gif or png.
- Photos should be square.
- Ideal pixel size is between 200 x 200 to 500 x 500, and should not to exceed 4000 in length or width.
- File size should not exceed 4MB.

Tip: For all LinkedIn images dimensions, see Appendix C.

Here are what I believe to be some effective profile photos on LinkedIn:

Ross Dabrow   3rd
VP & Co-Founder, Catch & Release, Inc. I Revenue Scaling Growth Expert I High Tech Sales & Digital Content Licensing
Greater New York City Area | Internet

Current   Catch & Release, Inc.
Previous   Corbis, T3Media (formerly Thought Equity Motion), Framepool, Inc.
Education University of Maryland College Park

[Connect] [Send Ross InMail ▼]   **500+**
                                         connections

Susan (Schmidt) Thomson   1st
Business Coach I Executive Coach I CEO I Chairman of the Board
Madison, Wisconsin Area | Management Consulting

Current   ActionCOACH Business Coaching, South Metropolitan Business Association
Previous   Kapro Tools, Inc., Fiskars Brands
Education University of South Carolina School of Journalism

[Send a message ▼]   **500+**
                                         connections

Note: Depending on your industry, you might choose to post a more or less formal photo. If you work in the music industry, perhaps you might choose a more colorful pose!

BACKGROUND IMAGE

To add a background image to your profile, begin with a 1400 × 425 pixel jpg image that depicts your brand. Go to your profile page by clicking on either Profile or Edit Profile from the menu:

At the top of your profile, click Edit Background.

Select one of the images provided or upload your own and save.

Here are what I believe to be some effective profile backgrounds on LinkedIn.

A Note About Privacy

You might have a concern that people could start harassing you due to your public photo. I myself have had a few people contact me under the guise of a professional connection when they seemed more interested in flirtation!

As an alternative to posting your photo publicly, you can set your Privacy settings so that your profile photo is only visible to those in your network (Go to Privacy & Settings, click on the Profile tab, and choose Change your profile photo & visibility). This step may deter someone from asking for a connection based on visual interests alone. However, the downside is that you lose the very important advantages of having a profile photo.

Profile	Privacy Controls	Settings
Communications	Turn on/off your activity broadcasts	Manage your Twitter settings
	Select who can see your activity feed	Manage your WeChat settings
Groups, Companies & Applications	Select what others see when you've viewed their profile	**Helpful Links**
	Turn on/off How You Rank	Edit your name, location & industry »
Account	Select who can see your connections	Edit your profile »
	Choose who can follow your updates	Edit your public profile »
	Change your profile photo & visibility »	Manage your recommendations »
	Show/hide "Viewers of this profile also viewed" box	
	Manage who you're blocking »	
	Manage who can discover you by your phone number »	

For more information on Privacy concerns, see Mistake #6.

A Note About Discrimination

Some people do not post a photo on LinkedIn because of concerns about age or race discrimination. Note that I can't give you legal advice. What I can say is that the reality is discrimination happens even though of course it is illegal. My question for you would be: Would you want to work for a company that doesn't contact you because of something they see in your picture? If they are going to discriminate, chances are they will do it in the interview if they don't have a chance to make judgments based on your photo. And the fact is, you will almost certainly be discriminated against for not posting a photo at all, since people are naturally more interested when they have a visual picture of the person they are contacting.

That said, if you are 50+ and concerned about age discrimination, it can't hurt to post a photo that makes you look as youthful as possible. Age is just a number, and your photo can give a sense of your energy and enthusiasm about your life and career!

Creating a Custom Background Image

There are several methods for creating a custom background image for your LinkedIn profile. Here are a few that I've discovered:

1. FOTOR

Go to Fotor.com and click on Collage. In the left sidebar, under "Border," click the lock icon to unlock the dimensions and change the size to 1400 x 425. From there you can create a tiled background using your own images. Here's an example:

For more on how to design a custom background image with Fotor, read their blog article on Fotor's Blog.[2]

2. PICMONKEY

PicMonkey.com has a collage feature that works similarly to Fotor's, however, you will need to crop the image to size after creating it. Begin by changing your canvas width to 1400, keeping in mind that the dimensions for your background are approximately 3:1 width to height. For example, you'll only be able to use bottom 1/3 of the "Biggie Small" collage option, rotated 90 degrees, and also the third "L-egant" option. See images below for reference.

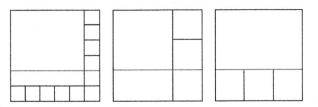

---

3. PIMAGIC

Pimatic[3] allows you to crop your image to the size needed. You'll need to begin with a photo that is 1400 x 425. Just drag the cursor to highlight and select the part of the images you'd like to use.

There are also many free photo editing software platforms out there that will allow you to create an image, including Paint.net and Editor by pixlr.com.

Results to Expect

According to Link for Small Business, "adding a profile photo could result in 14 times more views than someone without."

An engaging profile photo and background create a personal relationship with your viewers. You will be more likely to be contacted by many recruiters. People will see you as friendly and professional, and will be encouraged to read more about you. They might even be inspired to do business with you.

---

3 Pimagic - http://app.pikock.com/pimagic

MISTAKE #3

Profile Not 100% Complete

The Problem

If your profile is not complete, due to the way LinkedIn's search function works, you will not rank as highly in searches as others with 100% complete profiles; and you will be significantly less likely to generate interest for your profile. Plus, LinkedIn will keep bugging you with questions, egging you on to complete your profile every time you log in. This is one of the easiest items to handle, so why not do it?

There are five levels of profile strength, based on your level of completeness: Just beginning, Intermediate, Advanced, Expert and All Star. I'd like you to be an All-Star by the end of this book!

The Tune-Up

Complete your profile! LinkedIn reported on February 14, 2012 that the following items comprise a 100% complete profile, as listed on the Profile Completeness[1] page:

- Your industry and location (According to Link Humans, "adding an industry could get your 15 times more profile views."
- An up-to-date current position (with a description)
- Two past positions
- Your education (According to Link Humans, "members who have an education on their profile receive an average of 10 times more profile views than those who don't."
- Your skills (minimum of 3)
- A profile photo
- At least 50 connections

If you are not currently employed, you might be conflicted about what to list as your current position. There is no definitive answer to this question. The fact is, if your profile is 95% complete due to the lack of a current position, and you have taken all the other advice in this book, you will still do quite well in searches.

However, you might choose to list your job title as the position you are seeking, and your "company" as "--" or as "Open to New Opportunities." Some recruiters do search for that keyword phrase; however some recruiters are turned off by it. Also see Bonus Tip #4.

The good news is that your LinkedIn profile is a living document and you can always try something one way for a month or two, then try something different for another period.

---

1 Profile Completeness - http://tinyurl.com/l5axwtl

Results to Expect

You will rank more highly in searches and be designated an All-Star; your status will appear via this image on your profile!

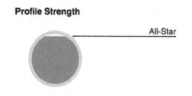

But that's just a label. According to LinkedIn, your profile will be 40 times more likely to be viewed if it is 100% complete, giving you 40 times the opportunities you want through LinkedIn! If you do not have a 100% complete profile, and if you want to start seeing bigger results, completing your profile is one of the easiest paths to a KILLER LinkedIn Profile!

MISTAKE #4

Websites Labeled Generically,
e.g. "Company Website" or "Personal Website"

In your Contact Info section, you can list up to three websites of your choice. The display of those websites can look like this:

> 🌐 Websites   My website: The Essay Expert
>   The Essay Expert Blog

But many people's Website sections look like this:

> 🌐 Website   Company Website
>   Company Website
>   Company Website

The Problem

Titles like "Company Website" don't brand your name or your company name. They are generic. They also do not reveal what exactly the link connects to. Why would anyone click without knowing where the link leads?

The Tune-Up

It's easy to personalize your website names. Just click on Contact Info at the bottom right of your top box. You will be brought to a screen where you will see the following:

Clicking on the pencil next to Websites will open a new window where you can add or edit up to three websites:

Websites

Other: ▼	My website: The Es:	http://www.TheEssayExpert.com	✕
Other: ▼	The Essay Expert B	http://www.TheEssayExpert.com/blog	✕
Choose... ▼	URL (ex: http://www.site.com)		✕

Save   Cancel

Under the Websites menu, choose Other. Then write in your specific website description. You might want to keep My Company and provide additional information, such as: "My Company: The Essay Expert."

If your company has a special landing page you want LinkedIn users to see, feel free to list that page as one of the three websites.

Another great option for sharing websites is to post them in your Publications or even your Projects section. See Mistake #13 for more information on the ever-important Special Sections.

 Publications

How to Write a KILLER LinkedIn Profile
Self-Published. #1 Top-Rated in Amazon's Business Writing Category
February 2012

Read this Best-Selling E-Book and Tune Up your LinkedIn Profile!

Are you getting the results that you want from your LinkedIn profile? If not, this book is for you. I provide you with 18 detailed strategies and writing tips that other "LinkedIn experts" don't cover. First I tell you how to get found on LinkedIn, and then I tell you how to keep people reading.

By following the advice in this... **more**

The Essay Expert Blog | Resumes | LinkedIn | Personal Statements
Brenda Bernstein | The Essay Expert LLC
March 2009

Weekly wisdom on resume, LinkedIn, personal statement and other writing topics from Brenda Bernstein, The Essay Expert!

How to Write a WINNING Resume: 50 Tips to Reach Your Job Search Target
The Essay Expert
September 2013

If you're eager to read a do-it-yourself resume guide that's easy-to-read, practical and up-to-date, this is the book you've been looking for! How to Write a WINNING Resume takes you through the resume writing process step by step, from thinking through your approach to creating a great format, crafting effective branding statements and bullets, and handling specific challenges.

Resume Tip: I credit this tip to a client who told me he had purchased his name.com domain and then pointed the domain to his LinkedIn page. If you don't already own yourname.com for other purposes, such as a blog or other job search marketing materials, this option might be a good one for you. For example, instead of listing your profile at the top of your resume as "https://www.linkedin.com/in/brendabernstein," you could write "LinkedIn profile: www.brendabernstein.com," which looks much cleaner and also shows that you are tech-savvy.

Results to Expect

People will be more likely to click on your website links because they know where the links lead! This translates into more interaction with your profile and possibly more career opportunities and sales.

Additionally, putting a link to your company's website on LinkedIn will boost the company's Google page rank.

MISTAKE #5

Public Profile URL (Link) with lots of Numbers, Letters and Slashes at the End

Your Public Profile URL is the link that brings people to your LinkedIn profile page. While in Edit Profile mode, you can see the name of the link at the bottom of the top box on your profile, right before the Activity section.

Here's mine:

in www.linkedin.com/in/brendabernstein/

The Problem

LinkedIn creates a Public Profile URL for you that contains lots of slashes and numbers at the end. All this gobbledygook (to use a technical term) prevents brand recognition. If you leave your Public URL as LinkedIn's default, your readers will be left with letters and numbers instead of your name. http://www.linkedin.com/in/brendabernstein/13/72a/a64 just isn't as memorable as http://www.linkedin.com/in/brendabernstein. It takes up a lot more room on your resume or business card too.

The Tune-Up

You can change your URL to a "vanity" URL that ends with your name by clicking on the URL at the bottom of your top box.

Brenda Bernstein

Resume & LinkedIn Profile Writer, Author, Speaker ★
Executive Resumes ★ Executive LinkedIn Profiles ★
College Essays

Madison, Wisconsin Area | Writing and Editing

Current	The Essay Expert, Kaplan, Inc.
Previous	University of Wisconsin Law School - Career Services, CAMBA Legal Services, CAMBA Tenant Support Services
Education	New York University School of Law

View profile as ▼

500+
connections

in https://www.linkedin.com/in/brendabernstein

Contact Info

When you click, you will land here:

At the top of the right-hand column you will see "Your Public Profile URL."

Click on the pencil icon and you reveal an entry field where you can customize away!

Is the name you want unavailable? Try your last name followed by your first name, or use an initial or two or a number. Find a solution that works for you! Keep in mind that your custom URL must be between 5 and 30 characters and may not include any spaces or "special characters" which include dashes, dots and other symbols.

Important Note: Once you change your Public Profile URL to a custom URL, your previous URL will no longer work. If you have your Public Profile URL on your resume, business card, e-mail signature or any other materials, change it to your new custom link on all these documents. If you have created a QR code that links to your LinkedIn Profile, you will need to change the QR code as well.

Keyword Tip: If you have room to add keywords at the end of your profile URL, you can get search engine optimization (SEO) mileage out of adding your top keyword directly after your name! For instance, johnjonescorporatecounsel or janesmithitdirector. Adding these keywords will not affect your search rankings within LinkedIn itself, but it will provide some leverage in Google searches.

Results to Expect

Your name will stand out at the end of the URL and provide a cleaner image on your resume, business cards, or anywhere else you are sharing your LinkedIn URL. Your Google search rankings will improve based on the inclusion of your name as well as keywords if space allows.

MISTAKE #6

Fewer than 500 Connections

The number of Connections you have appears in the lower right corner of your profile:

A LinkedIn poll conducted by Michael Field Pty Ltd[1] asked 1,006 LinkedIn members exactly how many connections they have.

The findings:

- 54% of respondents had less than 500 connections
- 27% had between 500-999
- 12% had between 1,000-1,999
- 3% had between 2,000-2,999
- 4% had 3,000+ connections

The Problem

Depending on your intention with your profile, you might be putting yourself at a big disadvantage by having fewer than 500 connections. Your updates will go to a limited audience; the people who view your profile might see you as "unconnected"; and, perhaps most important, you will often not appear in searches if you are not connected on at least a 2nd degree level to the people conducting the search.

In fact, someone could search for you by your actual name and not find you if you do not have at least a 2nd degree connection to that person! So it is absolutely critical that you increase your number of connections.

There are admittedly some advantages to having fewer connections, or at least to having carefully-chosen connections, as outlined in the article, Looking for a Job? Having Too Many Contacts on LinkedIn May Backfire.[2] This report, based on a limited study by The University of Texas at Austin, points out that if you want to increase your ability to obtain referrals, as opposed to just job leads, you must have a strong network of people who

1 How Many LinkedIn Connections Do Power Networkers Have? - http://tinyurl.com/mrsnren

2 Looking for a Job? Having Too Many Contacts on LinkedIn May Backfire - http://tinyurl.com/kjqvyto

know you well. I would suggest that a large network and a strong network are not mutually exclusive, and that every power LinkedIn user would benefit from building both.

Another reason to expand your network is that LinkedIn has made it more and more difficult to communicate with people who are not our 1st degree connections. You've probably experienced searching for someone and having results come up that suggest you must send InMail or subscribe to LinkedIn Premium in order to write to the person you're trying to reach. Perhaps even the person's last name is unavailable to you. And the Connect button is nowhere to be found! This is certainly a bind you want to get out of.

> **Note:** Recruiters using LinkedIn® Recruiter Talent Solutions have a different functionality on their searches. They receive results based on relevance, not on degree of connection. So having a small network will not hurt you if the person doing the search has a premium LinkedIn Corporate membership.

The Tune-Up

There is a balance to be struck between expanding your network as aggressively as possible and expanding it with quality connections. Your strategy will be different depending on your situation. If you are a CEO or Corporate Counsel or a VP of Asset Management at a Hedge Fund, you will make different choices than if you are an internet marketer or a resume writer. Choose your connections based on the image you want to project as well as your goal with your LinkedIn profile.

As a general rule, the more people you are connected with within your field or client base, the more leverage you will get from your connections. Additionally, the more connections your connections have, the more rapidly your network will expand.

One easy way to expand your network is to accept connection requests from people you know or whom you would want to know. Some professionals have a rule that they will only connect with someone after a phone call or in-person conversation. This practice is a great way to meet people in an authentic way and to create valuable alliances.

Following are some suggestions of ways to reach out yourself to expand your network responsibly. Choose the options that work best for you!

Your Address Book

There are many ways to build your network on LinkedIn. One easy method is to send requests to people in your address book. If they are already LinkedIn members, they will accept your invitation almost 100% of the time. If they are not members, many will join LinkedIn at your request, because they trust you and they've probably been thinking about joining for a long time anyway.

Click on Add Connections:

Here's the screen that will help you find people you already know:

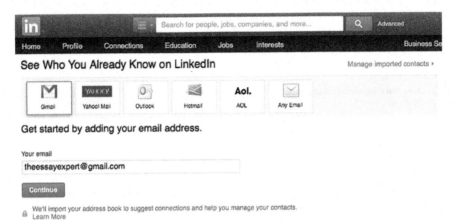

If you have an email account with any of the listed providers, you can enter your login information and you will get a list of people in your e-mail address book who are current members of LinkedIn.

> **IMPORTANT:** I do NOT recommend sending invitations to your contacts using this feature! The message that gets sent will be a generic message that says "[Contact's First Name], I'd like to add you to my professional network on LinkedIn. - [Your First Name]"

Instead, look at the list, note the people with whom you would like to connect, and send them a personal message. Since they are in your address book, you most definitely have their e-mail address, which you may need to provide.

Alumni

I also recommend using the Find Alumni tool from the Connections or Education menu drop-down so that you can connect with alumni from your educational institutions:

With this feature, you will have the opportunity to send invitations with personalized messages to each of your desired connections. You can invite a new connection to your network, or find those who are already 1st level connections. Use the right arrow key to find the "How you are connected" column and click on 1st Connections.

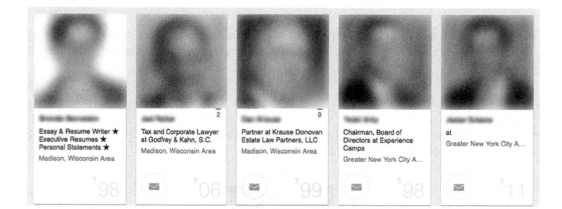

Then, click on the mail icon.

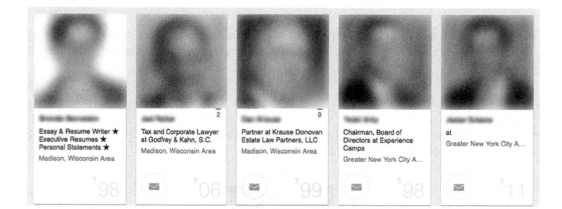

For more information on connecting with alumni, go to The Best Way to Network with Alumni on LinkedIn[3]. The feature is quite robust, allowing you to sort alumni by date, location, company, career, field of study, skills and connection level. Don't miss out on this opportunity to start up conversations with your fellow classmates; you have an automatic connection with them and they are likely to want to help you!

3 The Best Way to Network with Alumni on LinkedIn - http://tinyurl.com/cxtr326

Word of warning, especially for older job seekers: If you search for alumni by date and the person has not entered their dates of school attendance, you will not find them by searching with a date range. Similarly, if you do not enter your dates of education, you will not be found by your classmates if they search by date. You need to consider the benefits of hiding your age vs. the benefits of connecting with alumni from your class.

Group Members

Another important source of connections are your LinkedIn groups. If someone posts an interesting discussion or comment, compliment the person in your request to connect. You will be irresistible! The people in your LinkedIn groups are key players for you to connect with. They are most likely to be interested in connecting with people like you. And you can message them without needing to be officially connected first! Note that LinkedIn limits the number of 1:1 group member messages you can send to 15 per month.[4]

As I mentioned above, LinkedIn has a generic message you can send when you request a connection. DON'T DO IT!! Take the time to write a personal note to anyone you want to connect with. Wouldn't you appreciate the same courtesy?

Initiating a Connection the Right Way

When searching for someone to connect with, start by selecting People from the dropdown menu in the main search bar:

Then type in their name. If there are several profiles listed under that name, LinkedIn will return a list. DO NOT use the Connect button from this page if you want to send a customized message.

---

4 Communicating with a Fellow Group Member - http://tinyurl.com/naexcjr

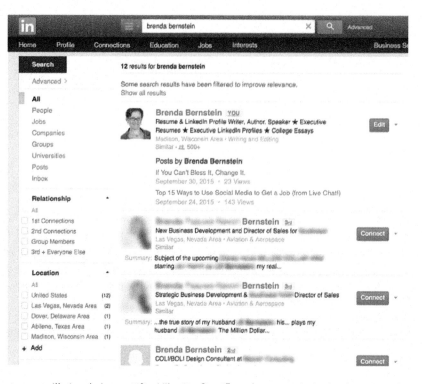

If you click Connect, you will simply be notified "Invite Sent" and a generic invitation containing no message at all will be delivered. Here is what your contact will see:

What would someone's incentive be for accepting such a generic invitation?

Instead, you can also go to that person's profile and either click the Connect button if they have one:

Or you may be able to hover over the Send [name] InMail **button and click** Connect.

If you do accidentally connect with someone without including a message, you can always send another message with a customized invitation later! This practice will come in handy if you connect with someone via your mobile phone, in which case you will not have an option to send a customized invitation.
You will then be taken to the following page:

Simply select your relationship to that person and change the message in the box. Easy!

Note that if you connect with someone via your mobile phone, you will not have an option to send a customized invitation. In this case, you can always send another message with a customized invitation later!

Here's a chance to practice . . . go to www.linkedin.com/in/brendabernstein/en and connect with me on LinkedIn!

You may very well find yourself staring at a page like this, where your only option is to provide the connection's email address:

Millie's email address:

⑦

Include a personal note: (optional)

I'd like to add you to my professional network on LinkedIn.

-Brenda B.

Important: Only invite people you know well and who know you. Find out why.

Send Invitation   or Cancel

According to the LinkedIn Help Center[5], an email address is needed for an invitation when:

- The recipient's email preferences are set to only receive invitations from members who know their email address.
- You've reached the limit of invitations you can send without email addresses to people you've identified as a "Friend" during the invitation process.
- A number of recipients have clicked "I don't know this person" after getting your invitations.

You may also be asked for a person's email address if you have already sent them an invitation and you are sending one for the second time.

> **Note:** Remember to include a personal note to remind people who you are and explain why you want to connect. You can do this when you click **Connect** from the following locations:
> - The member's profile
> - The People You May Know feature
> - Search results

When you want to connect with someone and don't have the person's email address, try the following:

1. Look in the person's LinkedIn profile. You might find an email address somewhere if you look carefully!
2. Look up the person's company on Google and see how the company addresses are created. If you see other people with addresses like SamA@ABC.com or PaulaD@ABC.com, you can be pretty sure of the address for your targeted contact.

Remember that other people are trying to connect with you too! Make it easy for them by setting your privacy settings so people don't need your address to connect with you. And for those who are asked to list your email address, put as many of your email addresses in the LinkedIn system as possible. Some of your connections might have an old email address or one you do not use very often. Listing multiple email addresses in your

---

5 **Email Address Needed for an Invitation** - https://help.linkedin.com/app/answers/detail/a_id/1239

contact information will increase the possibility that your past contacts will be able to connect. To do this, visit your Privacy & Settings, which you will find under your photo in the upper right hand corner of your homepage:

You will be asked to sign in. Then you will be brought to a screen where can change your Primary Email or add a new email address. Click on Change/Add to see the following:

When you add as many email addresses as possible, it will become much easier for people to contact you, no matter where they know you from.

Making a "Warm" Connection

As of January 29, 2014, LinkedIn has been rolling out the "How You're Connected" tool. This feature was created with the intention of helping you find commonalities between you and those you would like to connect with, as well as how your 1st tier connection may know them, so you can create a more personalized introduction request.

For more about this feature, read LinkedIn's Official Blog article, Seeing Who You Know and How You Know Them Just Got Easier With LinkedIn.[6]

Requesting an Introduction

Note that LinkedIn's new messaging center was being rolled out at the time of this publication. The functionality and/or availability of this feature may differ from what is depicted in this book. Please make sure to sign up for our e-book updates to get the most current information about this LinkedIn feature.

When you want to connect with a 2nd degree connection, it may be necessary to request an introduction. LinkedIn makes this process easy with its "How You're Connected" tool.

Search for that person using the main search bar. From their profile, scroll down the right sidebar to see a tree of how you are connected and if there might be someone you feel comfortable requesting the introduction through. Then click the Get introduced link.

For more on how to use the "Get introduced" feature, read LinkedIn Help Center's article, Requesting an Introduction.[7] Requesting an introduction may seem intimidating, but if your 1st degree contact knows both you and the person you would like to meet, they will likely be happy to make the connection. However, it's also possible that they don't know them, in which case, your request may be denied. Don't give up! You can try the other 1st degree contacts from your "How You're Connected" list. Remember, the more connections you have, the easier it will be to connect with almost anyone on LinkedIn.

What if I want to remove a connection?

If you add someone and start to question the wisdom of that connection (e.g., the person starts spamming you with advertisements or, shall we say, "love notes"), it's easy to remove them as a connection.

First, click on Connections.

---

6 Seeing Who You Know and How You Know Them Just Got Easier With LinkedIn - http://tinyurl.com/oyeh2vj

7 Requesting an Introduction - http://tinyurl.com/ppp9gra

You will be brought to this screen:

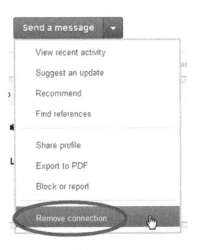

To remove a connection, scroll over the person's profile, click on the More button that appears, and select Remove Connection.

Alternately, you can visit any contact's actual profile and remove them using the dropdown menu next to the Send a message button:

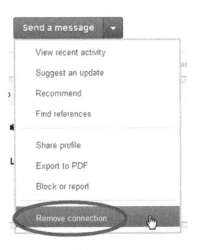

If you have an older (not upgraded) profile, to remove a connection follow the instructions on this page: Removing a Connection.[8]

Before You Find Yourself Needing to Remove a Connection . . .

If you want to make sure the person you're about to connect to is legit, you might like to try some of these detective-style methods recommended by my colleague, Rabbi R. Karpov, Ph.D.

---

8 Removing a Connection - https://help.linkedin.com/app/answers/detail/a_id/49

Before Linking, Perform Due Diligence

First, check out the photo (we learned this "Google Images" algorithm methodology from Robin Schlinger, several years ago).

1. Right click on any profile image and copy the image location.

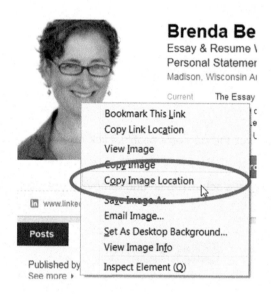

2. Next, run that photo through "Google Images" (https://images.google.com/). You can also find it by typing "google images" into your browser. Click the camera icon and paste in the image URL.

Now you can find some things out. Look for red flags:

a. Stock photo. That wholesome-looking woman, it turns out, wasn't really an Apple Computer VP . . . nor was that her profile!

b. Or worse: The photo is real, but it was stolen, either from someone living, such a military-man or Miss World Philippines contestant, or from someone deceased (hey, that's the late President of Zaire!)

Next, check out the rest of the general "picture":

1. Run the email address you find under the connection's Contact Info through Google. Did it come up as a known email address associated ONLY with a scammer/spammer?

2. Run the connection's name through Google. What turned up?

3. Run the name AND the email address through Google. Sometimes that is what turns up information that will make you glad you took this extra 5 minutes.

A Note about Privacy Concerns

Due to the upswing in number of complaints regarding LinkedIn users abusing their connected status to stalk other users, on February 20, 2014, LinkedIn implemented a member blocking feature.

You may have noticed that when you initiate a connection to a 2nd level party or greater, LinkedIn states:

Once you connect, your new connection has access to viewing people you know (if your settings are set the same way as 63% of LinkedIn users); reading every activity update you post; and sending items to your inbox.

Before the blocking feature was made available, a user's only recourse having encountered an unsavory connection, was to disconnect with that person. Blocking a member allows you to completely remove your profile from that connection's view, and theirs from yours. In addition, says LinkedIn:

- You won't be able to message each other on LinkedIn
- If you're connected, you won't be connected anymore
- We'll remove any endorsements and recommendations from that member
- You won't see each other in your "Who's Viewed Your Profile"
- We'll stop suggesting you to each other in features such as "People You May Know" and "People also Viewed"

To block someone, visit their profile and hover over the down arrow to the right of the message button and click Block or report.

You will then get a popup window with options to block this person or report them or both. If you choose to report them, you will need to provide a reason for doing so. Note that you do not need to disconnect from your contact first; blocking them automatically disconnects you.

Once you have blocked someone, their name will appear on your block list. You can view the list by visiting your Privacy & Settings under Manage who you're blocking. From here you can also unblock members, should you choose to do so.

For more information on how the blocking feature works, including how to block from within a group environment, read LinkedIn Help's Member Blocking - Overview.[9]

Of course, ideally we would never want to have to block anyone, so here are a few things you can do to protect your privacy in the first place:

1. Only accept connections from people you know. LinkedIn is a great supporter of this philosophy; however, there is a trade-off between maintaining a small number of reputable connections and broadening your network (and thus increasing your leads) by connecting with people outside of your circle.

2. Change your settings under Privacy & Settings so that only those who know your email address or are in your imported contacts list can send you invitations (Go to Privacy & Settings, Communications tab, and click on Select who can send you invitations). (For more details on how to find the Privacy & Settings section, see Mistake #18.)

3. To protect the privacy of your connections, go to Privacy & Settings, Profile tab, and click on Select who can see your connections where you will have an option to prevent others from seeing see your network. This will prevent your 1st degree connections from seeing exactly how many connections you have; otherwise they will be able to get past the "500+" and see both your exact number of connections and who those connections are.

---

9 Member Blocking - Overview - http://tinyurl.com/mp9vdvj

Profile	Privacy Controls	Settings
Communications	Turn on/off your activity broadcasts	Manage your Twitter settings
	Select who can see your activity feed	Manage your WeChat settings
Groups, Companies & Applications	Select what others see when you've viewed their profile	**Helpful Links**
	Turn on/off How You Rank	Edit your name, location & industry »
Account	Select who can see your connections	Edit your profile »
	Choose who can follow your updates	Edit your public profile »
	Change your profile photo & visibility »	Manage your recommendations »
	Show/hide "Viewers of this profile also viewed" box	
	Manage who you're blocking »	
	Manage who can discover you by your phone number »	

None of these alternative actions is a perfect solution. If you encounter unwanted attention on LinkedIn, it is your prerogative to block them. You may also want to report any harassment to LinkedIn Corporation; and if necessary, please seek legal counsel.

Connected . . . Now What?

Once someone accepts your connection request, you have the opportunity to communicate with that person!

If you are a job seeker, you might want to ask your new connection for advice on whom you might approach to further your job search.

When you send a message through LinkedIn mail, you can attach files to your reply, so you might choose to forward a copy of your resume or other marketing materials!

I do **not** recommend sending emails to all your connections stating that you are a job seeker and asking them if they know of any openings. This type of email will be quickly forgotten at best, and result in a spam report at worst.

Similarly, if you are a business owner, do **not** send out unsolicited requests for business to your contacts. Instead, thank them for their connection, and perhaps send them an article you think they will like, comment on something you were impressed by in their profile, ask them a great question about their business, or even mention someone in your network with whom they might want to connect. If you think it would be useful, go ahead and set up a phone or in-person meeting!

In short, use your networks wisely and politely. The right approach will reap big rewards.

Once your network starts to grow, you will start receiving messages through LinkedIn. If you're not in the habit of logging into your account daily, be sure you set your email frequency under Privacy & Settings to receive individual emails for each message you get from a connection:

Messages from other members
Invitations, messages, and other communication from LinkedIn members

Invitations to connect	Individual Email ▼
Invitations to join groups	Individual Email ▼
Messages from connections	Individual Email ▼
InMails, introductions and Open Profile messages	Individual Email ▼
New connection suggestions	Individual Email ▼
Profiles sent to you	No Email ▼
Job suggestions from connections	No Email ▼

Save changes   Cancel

Note that messages coming from LinkedIn might sometimes get caught by your spam filter, and if you use Gmail, messages from connections can get filtered into the "Social" category, so be sure to check these places often and don't miss that next opportunity!

Two great ways to keep in touch with your connections are by congratulating them on their successes and wishing them a happy birthday. A simple human connection often leads to a deeper conversation! Start by checking up on what's happening in their lives with the Keep in Touch option under the Connections tab:

Connections   Educ
Keep in Touch
Add Connections
Find Alumni

On the Keep in Touch page you will see the recent happy events in your connections' lives. Go ahead. Reach out! Just click the message link below the connection you want to wish well:

Add your customized note and hit Comment.

Most important, don't be afraid to pick up the phone and talk to your new connections in real time.

Start up a conversation and you will learn much more than you could ever gather from their profile.

Staying organized for future contact.

LinkedIn offers you the option to set up a reminder to reach out to that person in one day, one week or one month (sorry, specific dates cannot be selected—perhaps LinkedIn will add this in the future!). From your contact's profile, click on the Relationship tab and then select the Reminder option.

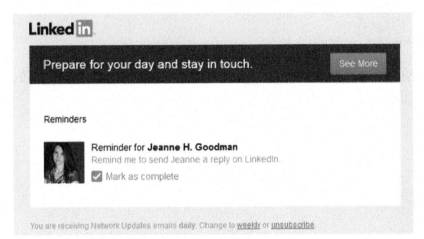

The reminder will show up in your inbox and look something like this:

You can view all of your reminders by clicking on Keep in Touch under the Connections tab.

Organizing Your Connections

For even more organizational power, use the tagging feature. Tagging is a way to filter your connections according to categories/keywords that you establish. You can create up to 200 unique tags. To assign, add or delete tags, from your Connections page, click the Tag link under any contact's profile.

Jeanne H. Goodman 1st   1 day ago   in
Virtual Assistant and Website Technician at Life Liberty VA
Rochester, New York Area
● Tag ✉ Message More ▾

You can then select the tag you'd like to associate with that connection.

To add a new tag, scroll to the end of your list and click Add New Tags. To edit or delete a tag, click Manage Tags.

Here are some of mine:

● Tag ✉ Message More ▾

☐ attorneys
☐ career services
☐ classmates
☐ clients
☐ colleagues
☐ family
☐ favorites
☐ friends
☐ group members
☐ landmark
☐ law students
☐ madison
☐ partners
☐ potential clients
☐ recruiters
☐ service providers
☐ webinar participants

＋ Add New Tags
⚙ Manage Tags

You can also utilize the Relationship feature to tag someone. Just visit that contact's profile, and on the Relationship tab, click the Tag icon. Then select the group you want to add your contact to. Also, by clicking the plus icon, you can write notes, set up reminders to follow up with that contact, and track of details on how you met, all in one convenient place.

Of course the first step in organizing your connections is making them in the first place. Are you feeling hesitant about reaching out to people in your groups and networks? Well, this is not the time to be shy! You might be surprised by how many people will be happy to connect with you.

Results to Expect

By increasing your number of connections, you will be much more likely to appear at the top of searches. You will have more views of your page each day and each week. More people will request to connect with you because of whom you know. And you'll eventually be able to impress your viewers with that coveted "500+" connections listing on your profile!

How do you know how much activity is occurring in your account? Go to your homepage and look near the top of the page.

If you click on the box with the number of people who have viewed your profile in the past day, you will be brought to a screen with a list of your most recent visitors and a graph of how often people viewed you over the past 90 days.

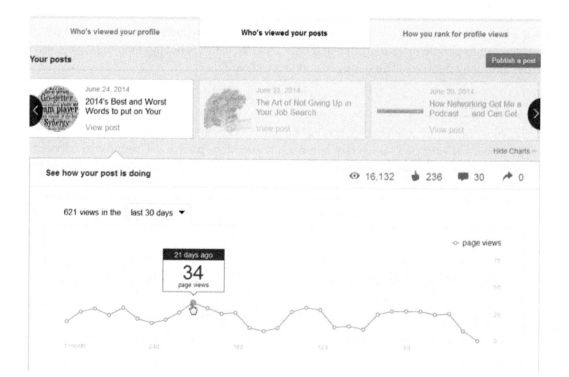

Clicking on the Who's viewed your posts tab will reveal analytics for the long-form posts you've published. Sliding to the article you'd like to review will tell you how it has fared amongst your readers over the last week, 2 weeks, month, 6 months and year. Hovering over the line on the graph reveals the actual views on that date.

Scroll down to see the profiles of those who have commented on your article, to read their comments and to connect.

Perhaps most importantly, you can view the demographics of your readers, allowing you to determine which keywords and topics they searched most, how they found your article, where they live and what industry they are in.

Demographics of your readers ⊙

Top 4 industries		**Top 4 job titles**		**Top 4 locations**		**Top 4 traffic sources**
19% Marketing and Advertising		14% Salesperson		16% Greater New York City Ar…		97% Google Search
15% Information Technology …		13% Marketing Specialist		12% San Francisco Bay Area		1% LinkedIn Pulse
9% Financial Services		8% Project Manager		8% Washington D.C. Metro …		1% LinkedIn.com
6% Higher Education		7% Research / Graduate As…		7% Greater Los Angeles Area		

Who's responding to your post   Likes (236)   **Comments (30)**

You can also view how your profile has ranked among your connections over the past 30 days. Select the How you rank for profile views **tab:**

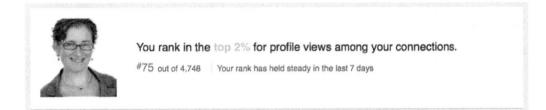

> **You rank in the** top 2% **for profile views among your connections.**
>
> #75 out of 4,748   │   Your rank has held steady in the last 7 days

For more details on how the "How Your Rank" feature can be used by job seekers, business owners, student and sales professionals, read LinkedIn's office blog article, Make the Most of Who's Viewing Your LinkedIn Profile with 'How You Rank'.[10]

Follow the advice in this book and watch your numbers soar! Here are the results one reader produced from implementing my suggestions:

Trends

Views Appearances in Search

10 Make the Most of Who's Viewing Your LinkedIn Profile with 'How You Rank' - http://tinyurl.com/kq5g9cu

According to Greig Wells of BefoundJobs.com, if you are a job seeker you will get one job offer for every 300 views to your account. That means if you get 10 views a day you will likely receive a job offer within one month!!

One survey[11] confirmed that 70.6% of LinkedIn members said the "Who's Viewed Your Profile" feature was one of the most helpful tools on LinkedIn. If you are a job seeker, knowing what employers or recruiters have been visiting your profile can guide you to follow up with those individuals. You might say something like, "I noticed you viewed my profile. I am very interested in x and would like to have a conversation with you this week or next. Might we set up time to meet?"

Want more information about Who's Viewed Your Profile?

With a free LinkedIn account, you're limited in how many people per day you can see who have viewed your profile; plus if you want to know details, you will get a result that says something like, "Someone in the Human Resources industry from Greater Denver Area."

For more detailed information about your viewers, as well as the ability to sort them in various ways and discover exactly how they found you, you must upgrade to LinkedIn Premium (LinkedIn Corporation will encourage you in multiple ways to do so).

Be forewarned that due to limitations members put on their profiles with their privacy settings, you might still run into roadblocks in trying to find out who has been visiting your profile; but you might get some information you would not otherwise be able to access.

---

11 Is LinkedIn Really Helping People? - http://tinyurl.com/qflwady

Writing and Presentation Tips for Your KILLER LinkedIn Profile

I'm about to make suggestions that might inspire you to change some sections of your profile. If you don't want these changes announced to all your connections, **turn off your activity updates**. Do this a day before you make the changes to give LinkedIn time to integrate them. While an announcement might still go out when you turn your activity updates back on, your connections will not receive notifications of every change you make while your notifications are off.

To turn off your activity broadcasts, go to Privacy & Settings:

At this point you may be required to enter your password again before proceeding. You will then be taken to the Privacy & Settings page. On the Profile tab you will see the option Turn on/off your activity broadcasts:

Uncheck the box and Save changes:

If you would like to share or hide your profile updates on a change-by-change basis, you can do so from your profile editing sidebar. Before saving your change, just select whether you would like to notify your network:

Prior to LinkedIn's adding this feature, if you wanted to make a simple change, you needed to go to your Privacy & Settings and turn off your activity broadcasts, make your changes, then go back and turn them on again.

Now you can make all of your changes privately!

MISTAKE #7

Blank or Ineffective Summary Section

The Summary section is your first opportunity to write a bio or other statement about who you are. It will get people interested in who you are and what you have to offer. It is your chance to show what makes you unique and desirable. It's also your chance to give context to the rest of your profile. You have 2000 characters to work with in this section.

The Problem

Leaving the Summary section blank leaves your readers with no background, and maybe no reason to read further. Writing long blocky paragraphs or a generally dull Summary will bore your readers at best, and turn them off at worst.

One common error is copying the Summary section from your resume straight into your LinkedIn profile. If you do this, you miss out on a chance to tell your story in 2000 characters. A copy and paste job will look exactly like a copy and paste job. I invite you to see some samples of how to do it differently on my LinkedIn Summary samples page, http://theessayexpert.com/samples/linkedin-profiles/.

Another common mistake I see people make in their LinkedIn profiles is that they do not distinguish who *they* are from who their *company* is. I call this "conflating" yourself with your company.[1] It leaves your readers confused.

> **Important:** If your Summary does not utilize the 2,000 characters allotted, you miss out on a chance to include keywords that can make you appear more frequently in searches. Don't let that opportunity go!

The Tune-Up

Write a keyword-rich Summary that makes your audience want to know more about you. It can be an engaging bio or other well-written statement about your strengths, skills and accomplishments, and what you have to contribute to your intended audience. Make sure you are gearing this statement toward your targeted readers. If you aren't sure of your target audience, it might be because you are unclear of your direction, or because you have two very disparate audiences—in which case you might not be ready to write a Summary at all.

---

1 Your LinkedIn Profile Summary: How to Distinguish Yourself from Your Company - http://tinyurl.com/m6j45p5

My only rules about the LinkedIn Summary section, if you choose to write one, are to gear it toward your intended audience and make sure it expresses who you are and what you have to offer. Other than that, take my advice or leave it, depending on what works for you.

Some questions you might want to answer in your LinkedIn Summary include:

- How did you get to where you are professionally?
- What are your top 3 accomplishments?
- What is the most important thing your audience should know about you and/or your company?
- What makes you different than others who do the same type of work?
- What action do you want people to take after reading your Summary?

Again, and I can't emphasize this enough: Direct your Summary to your audience! You would write something very different to target a potential employer than you would to target a potential client.

Following are some issues that might come up as you are writing your LinkedIn Summary, and some ideas of how to address them.

1st or 3rd Person?

Most LinkedIn Summaries are written in the first person ("I"), which makes them more personal and conversational. Some higher-level executives prefer to write in the 3rd person ("He" or "She"). In the end, this is your decision. Look at some profiles similar to yours and see what you like best!

Regardless of whether you write in first or third person, your Summary must express who you are as a *person*. Your company website, your LinkedIn Company page and even the LinkedIn Experience section are available for reporting information about your company. Your Summary is there for LinkedIn members to learn more about *you*!

How to Start?

I often choose to start the Summary section with a sub-headline. Even though you have a headline for your profile, attention spans are short so it can't hurt to remind people of who you are. Don't use the exact wording from your headline; instead create something new that includes keywords and a tagline. While this is not a rule, it's a trick to put in your toolbox.

EXAMPLE #1:　**IT Professional**

Headline:
Senior Software Architect I Systems Automation I Cloud Solutions I Systems Management / Integration I Data Management

Summary Intro:
SENIOR SYSTEMS ANALYST AND PROGRAMMER WITH LINUX AND CLOUD SOLUTIONS EXPERTISE

EXAMPLE #2: **Compliance Executive**

Headline:
INTERNATIONAL COMPLIANCE EXECUTIVE | Risk Management | Investigation
Leadership | Compliance Strategies | Loss Control

Summary Intro:
11 YEARS OF OPERATIONAL TURNAROUNDS, REVENUE GROWTH, FRAUD/WASTE
CONTROL AND COST-CUTTING | EMEA, NORTH AMERICA, AND LATIN AMERICA.

Following this headline you have many choices.

You might choose to list some of your compentencies. For example:

GLOBAL FINANCE EXECUTIVE AND ENTREPRENEUR with 20 years' success in
opening new markets, creating new services, and building new companies.

Product Development • Key Decision Maker Relationships • Market and Regulatory Trends
• Emerging Markets • Process Development • Strategies

Or you might choose to dive right into your history:

I am a Ph.D. candidate in Computer Engineering with 12+ years of systems architecture
design, software development, and process enhancement experience in the US and
abroad. A strategic and informed risk taker, I am an effective project manager and the "go-
to" choice to analyze complex problems and identify actionable processes.

OR, if using 3rd person:

SENIOR-LEVEL MANAGER & CAPACITY BUILDER • SITE REPLICATION EXPERT •
PROVEN LEADER OF PEOPLE & PROJECTS

Michelle Henry has almost 20 years of progressive experience in business, community,
and program development and cultivates prosperous organizations. She recently served
as Senior Vice President at a large, national non-profit and has held positions with United
Way of NYC and the Center for Alternative Sentencing & Employment Services.

I have seen effective profiles that begin with a quotation. For instance, this one from Eric Schmidt, VP of
Business Technology at Spacesaver Corporation:

"You need to be constantly reinventing. You need to challenge things. You need to try
different ideas, different technologies, different creative approaches. Because the world is
changing."

— Miles Nadal.

That quote is very representative of my career . . .

There is no hard and fast rule about how to start your profile. Choose a strategy and style that works for you!

Run-On Sentences

Run-on sentences can leave us both out of breath and confused. It's worth taking some time to write a Summary that comes across clearly and concisely. Use powerful language and correct grammar. It makes a difference.

You vs. Your Company

One of the biggest mistakes I see in LinkedIn summaries is the tendency for business owners to mix up who they are and who their company is. They might, for instance, write one sentence about the company followed by a sentence about themselves. The reader is left confused.

Here's an example of someone named Michael Phelps (no, not the swimmer) who does a great job of distinguishing himself from his company, and who succeeds in selling both:

> I am a research professional and LinkedIn trainer with more than eight years of combined market intelligence, competitive intelligence and Internet recruiting experience. My focus has been on deep web sourcing, executive interviews and online networking through social media. I've spoken at more than 60 events to hundreds of business professionals about the power of LinkedIn!

See how this entire paragraph is about the person himself? It works! We're right there with him! His second section reads as follows:

> Current Phelps Research Services Initiatives:
>
> *Selling and conducting targeted business research to help Wisconsin-based sales teams utilize market, competitive and prospect information to customize approaches to their clients.
>
> *Selling and conducting customized LinkedIn training to sales, marketing legal, HR, public relations, consulting, research and training teams.

Phelps clearly makes a switch from talking about himself to talking about his company. We understand, since his last name is Phelps, that he is the principal in the company and that he is behind these initiatives. We stay engaged and want to read more.

Here's another example of a business owner who writes about himself while still making it clear what his company offers:

> LEADERSHIP DEVELOPMENT · BUSINESS STRATEGY · MANAGEMENT CONSULTING
>
> Is your business poised to blast above your current expectations? Are you ready to take action to heighten your leadership performance?
>
> For more than two decades, I have helped executives improve success ratios, productivity, ROI and ROE. My clients include Fortune 500 companies such as Crown Holdings, IBM, and Time Warner, as well as many smaller business entities.

When problems and obstacles go unsolved, they prevent optimal operations and results. Asking and answering precisely the right questions is sometimes all it takes to develop a leader's ability to identify and resolve a business dilemma.

That's where I step in. In addition to consulting and mentoring executives and entrepreneurs, I have served as CEO of four companies, where I have improved leadership practices, implemented significant efficiencies, increased lines of credit, and preserved relationships through pragmatic and compassionate management.

My unique and confidential approach of guided dialogue and best practices teaches leaders to lead themselves so they get their careers back on track. Work with me to work smarter. Reduce stress by conquering challenges such as . . .

- Distractions
- Low Productivity
- Employee Retention
- Overdue Work
- Out-of-control Budgets
- Mismanaged Projects

Leaders who manage these issues in turn drive their company to solve problems and create higher levels of individual and organizational productivity. Most important, they become free to enjoy business again.

For more information about my company [Company Name], please visit [Web address] or read my book, Stop Telling . . . Start Leading! The Art of Managing People by Asking Questions.

When you are ready to take action to improve your leadership performance, call 555.555.1234 for a conversation about your requirements.

Confidential Job Search?

If you are engaged in a confidential job search, it is essential that your LinkedIn Summary does not make you look like a job seeker. I am unable to share specific examples of profiles for confidential job seekers, for obvious reasons. However here are some things to keep in mind and some guidelines to follow:

1. Remember, recruiters love passive job seekers! If you write a profile that sells your current company well, makes it clear you are happy and thriving in your current position, and includes effective keywords, guess what? You WILL be contacted by recruiters. And you could make your current employer happy as well — maybe even attract new clients and

2. Turn off your activity broadcasts before making any changes. Please see Mistake #18 for instructions on how to change your privacy settings so that you do not announce to the whole world that you have changed your profile. Yes, many employers see changes in your profile as a sign that you might be looking; so if this is not cool with your current employer, turn off your notifications!

3. You might want to stick with talking about what you do for your current company. The more emphasis you put on what you're currently doing, the more you will benefit your current employer.

4. You can also go with a general bio format. Just talk about where you've come from and how you got to where you are now.

5. Limit the number of "accomplishment" bullets in your Summary. Bullets of accomplishments scream out "resume" and might raise suspicion.

Let's Get Personal

Some of the best profile summaries highlight the personalities of the people writing them. Here are some samples that stood out to me for their creative approach!

EXAMPLE #1: **Anna Wang, Quota-Beating Sales Rep** (check out her last line!)

 Summary

Quota Beating, Award Winning Sales Rep

I am an extremely effective communicator, and an incredibly fast learner. I enjoy rising to new challenges, and I thrive in a competitive sales environment.

I close deals.

I have an innate ability to read between the lines and identify the needs of my customers, allowing me to consistently exceed quotas with my high close ratio and high rate of account retention.

When training reps in the field, I can quickly spot their weaknesses, and devise an immediately actionable plan to increase their close ratio.

As an ADM at American Marketing & Publishing selling four days a week, I broke $300K in revenue in 2013 to rank in the top 5% of reps nationwide in 2013.

I am currently a sales rep for GSK, calling on the UW Health IDN.

EXAMPLE #2: Jess Hornyak, Marketing Director

 Summary

When I was little, I wanted to drive a garbage truck. Then, I moved to Wisconsin and declared I would be the next Green Bay Packers QB once Brett Favre retired.

No one ever told me "No" (or that girls don't play in the NFL), but soon after I found art and writing, and hopes of being the next big name in football were passed along to Aaron Rodgers.

Ever since I've been immersed in the arts: from Saturday morning watercolor lessons and hand-made art projects for my friends' birthday gifts, to falling in love with writing and producing a novel for an 8th grade project and a minor in creative writing from a Big Ten school.

I've filled just as many notebooks with poems and imaginative free writing exercises as I have canvases with brush strokes.

I'm also practical. I make lists. I played three sports since I was three, and learned from a young age how to manage my time. I hated losing, and still do. Saying I'm competitive is an understatement. I want to give my best all the time, in hopes of inspiring others to be better too. And, not only am I a team player as a result, but I've come to believe that being a team player is at the center of any type of success. Because it's true when they say that two minds are better than one.

Therefore, it's safe to say I don't fit into a traditional bubble. I'm an art director, but I'm really so much more. I'm a strategist. A writer. An artist. A competitor. It's why I'm looking for people who could use a little more non-traditional in their everyday lives.

Plus, it means I'm never bored. And definitely not boring.

I moved to Austin, Texas to get a Masters degree and complete the prestigious Texas Creative sequence. I have two degrees and ample real-world experience. Now, I just need a place to use it.

Specialties:adobe photoshop, advertising, brand management, brochure design, budgeting, closing, coaching, concept development, customer service, development, dreamweaver, illustrator, indesign, microsoft excel, microsoft powerpoint, microsoft word, persuasion, web site production,

How would you express your true self in your LinkedIn Summary? It might not look like either of the above examples, and, in fact, it shouldn't! If you're inspired to get creative, find your own expression and go for it! Remember to include as many keywords as you can in the process.

What Makes a Good Call to Action? And Should I Include Contact Info?

If you want readers of your profile to take action, then tell them so! Ask them to contact you if you want to enter into conversations about a particular topic. Tell them that you can create results like the ones reported in your profile for their company.

If you are in a confidential job search, your best call to action would be something relating to your current company – perhaps an action for a potential client to take.

EXAMPLE #1:

If you would like to connect with a top-level cross-functional leader on the forefront of global business technology, particularly the industry shift to Cloud Services and Channel Incentives models, send me an invite!

EXAMPLE #2:

I am available for a leadership role where I can leverage my expertise to build new brands and transform businesses for rapid growth.

SET UP A FREE CONSULTATION TODAY!

Should you include contact information in your Summary? If you are a job seeker wanting recruiters to access your contact information easily, then YES, include your contact information in the first 50 words of your Summary. Why? Because the list view generated by LinkedIn Recruiter displays the beginning of your Summary section. If your contact information shows up in the list view, recruiters will be more likely to contact you.

For anyone not targeting recruiters, you may still choose to include contact information in your Summary, but you also have the option to include this information in the Contact Information section, so double dipping is not necessary. If you do include your email address, consider writing [at] instead of @ so that spambots won't be able to find your address easily.

Name with Common Misspellings?

If you have a commonly misspelled name, include common misspellings in your Summary. So if your name is Izabela Tomkins, include in your summary a line that says "Izabela Tomkins, AKA Isabella Thompkins." That way you will appear in searches for common misspellings of your name!

Other Special Issues?

For samples from the LinkedIn Official Blog of possible ways to approach career changes and other gaps on your LinkedIn profile, see their presentation on SlideShare, Representing your unique career path on your LinkedIn profile:

(http://www.slideshare.net/linkedin/representing-unique-career-paths-on-linkedin)

Even with all these topics and suggestions addressed, you may have a career history that requires individual attention. Don't be afraid to ask friends, colleagues or other professionals for assistance and feedback.

Results to Expect

A well written or even creatively written Summary tells the world that you are taking control over your personal brand. By powerfully stating who you are and what you have to offer up front, you will encourage more people to read your full profile. Add to that a solid showing of keywords, and more people will find you when they perform advanced searches. A well-directed and well-placed call to action is the final ingredient and is likely to inspire more people to pick up the phone or send you an email.

According to Link Humans, "a summary of 40 words or more makes you more likely to turn up in a future employer's search." And LinkedIn Small Business states that profiles with summaries get 10 times more views. Your Summary CAN be the section that gets you a job or a new customer! It is not a section to be ignored.

Samples

For samples of LinkedIn Summary sections from one The Essay Expert's clients, see http://theessayexpert.com/samples/linkedin-profiles/. You might also like my blog article, 3 Reasons NOT to copy your resume summary into your LinkedIn Summary section.[2]

Following are some additional LinkedIn Profile Summaries by The Essay Expert. These samples are geared toward the U.S. job market where a strong sell is appropriate; adjust accordingly based on your target country.

---

2 3 Reasons NOT to copy your resume summary into your LinkedIn® Summary section - http://tinyurl.com/kaj3t4y

EXAMPLE #1

 Summary

LAUNCHING / TRANSFORMING BUSINESSES DOMESTICALLY AND INTERNATIONALLY

✔ Building #1 sales organizations.

With a servant leadership philosophy, I have repeatedly proven that when sales executives invest in assembling and training teams of emotionally intelligent strategic thinkers aligned with the company vision, revenue & sales performance follow.

After 13 years of driving explosive growth in digital / online media—most recently as VP of N.American Sales at Corbis, a Bill Gates company, a global photography & video licensing leader—I know what it takes to rescue failing businesses, achieve 180-degree turnarounds and guide startups to market dominance in E-Commerce & B2B environments.

✔ Applying high-velocity, decisive business leadership when organizations need to power launches or overcome a crisis.

After delivering historic-level sales at Getty Images, I was recruited by Thought Equity Motion and positioned this no-name startup to ▶ overpower the top 2 industry players and ascend to market leadership in our initial 24 months sales-startup. After 5 years at other firms, I was re-recruited and ▶ transformed their troubled Eastern sales operation into the highest-performing region in 1 year.

✔ Channeling forward-thinking creativity into YoY revenue growth.

At Framepool, a German media rights company with no U.S. brand awareness, I optimized tight resources to pioneer a product that offset flatlining sales and attracted formerly elusive ad agency business. We converted every single customer-facing meeting into sales, ▶ outdistanced 4 formidable competitors to earn "preferred vendor" status and ▶ realized triple-digit growth in 3 years.

EXAMPLE #2

 Summary

TENACIOUS, PERFORMANCE-DRIVEN CUSTOMS BROKERAGE LEADER - Streamlining processes and providing the highest level of service to customers.

Since 1996 I have been with Norman G. Jensen, Inc. (NGJ), a major provider of U.S. and Canadian customs brokerage, freight forwarding, warehousing, distribution, and consulting services to thousands of North American importers and exporters. During this time I have built a well-rounded background that touches all facets of the business in an Automated Commercial Environment.

EXCELLENCE AT NGJ

► At NGJ, we take great pride in adding value to our customers' cross-border trade by ensuring that their products are smoothly and expeditiously moved across the borders of North America.
► We provide the most complete U.S./Canadian border coverage in the industry, as well as an impressive array of software solutions for small, medium, and large importers and exporters.

Currently I am the Southern Border Regional Manager and Automation & Centralization Director of our processing center in Sioux Falls, SD, where I manage all electronic customer communications and play a key role in directing operations, production, customer service, and new business development. I am able to talk to a farmer in the field about the most efficient way to get his product across the border and am equally comfortable making a presentation on process improvements to Senior Executives.

INNOVATION AND EFFICIENCY CONTRIBUTIONS:

► Initiated, presented, and directed the implementation of process improvements from cradle to grave, including the development of software to improve processes for cross-border trade.
► Using my unique ability to work the simplest task through to the end product, whether it is a project or procedures, I am skilled at developing software and procedures that save time and reduce costs in international trade.

When you need an expert in the customer brokerage industry, contact me at ─ ████████
████████████

EXAMPLE #3

 ## Summary

SENIOR-LEVEL MANAGER & CAPACITY BUILDER ◆ SITE REPLICATION EXPERT ◆ PROVEN LEADER OF PEOPLE & PROJECTS

▇▇▇▇▇▇▇▇ has almost 20 years of progressive experience in business, community, and program development and cultivates prosperous organizations. She recently served as Senior Vice President at a large, national non-profit and has held positions with United Way of NYC and the Center for Alternative Sentencing & Employment Services.

▇▇▇▇▇ success is derived from her abilities to leverage stakeholder relationships; manage multi-city initiatives; develop partnerships; and achieve results through innovation. She takes a project from zero to full speed ahead, fostering high-performing teams and uniting senior management. Her unique ability to build capacities of scale ensures fiscal responsibility and business growth.

Demonstrating leadership in community service is also a priority for ▇▇▇▇. She served as Chair of the Board at the Center for Community Alternatives and currently contributes as a Board Member on CCA's audit committee. Further, she has presented on benefits access at national conferences.

CAREER HIGHLIGHTS:
◆ PROGRAM GROWTH—Replicated proven benefits access model that originated in New York and expanded it across 8 states.

◆ FISCAL MANAGEMENT—Oversaw $14 million government- and private-sector-funded portfolio of work support programs, including public and private benefits, housing and foreclosure mitigation, and conditional cash transfers.

◆ PERFORMANCE MANAGEMENT—Managed more than 40 employees, volunteers and consultants to collectively deliver vital services to low income workers and their families.

◆ CAPACITY BUILDING—Increased capacity of nonprofits nationally to integrate benefits access services into their program designs.

Organizations searching for a transformative leader will find their ideal candidate in ▇▇▇▇▇▇

EMAIL: ▇▇▇▇▇▇▇▇▇▇▇▇

EXAMPLE #4:

 Summary

Commissioning Startup Engineer I Full Cycle Project Management I Hands-on Technical Expertise I Matrix Team Leadership I RFP Response I Troubleshooting I Dispute Resolution I Customer Satisfaction I Cost & Revenue Optimization I Budget & Resource Management I HVAC I Boilers I Marine Diesell Electrical Systems I Automation

LARGE POWER PROJECT COMMISSIONING/STARTUP
√ Georgia Pacific Port Hudson: 1.2M lbs/hr (Process)
√ Roquette America: 630,000M lbs/hr (Process)
√ Howe Sound Pulp and Paper: 280,000M lbs/hr (Process)
√ Gainesville Renewable Energy Center: 100 MWE

FULL-CYCLE PROJECT MANAGEMENT: RFP, NEGOTIATIONS, DELIVERY
√ $100K building automation system digital controller design/upgrade for lower utility costs.
√ Solid chemical Nalco 3D Tracer system installation with 18-month payback.

TROUBLESHOOTING & REPAIRS
√ Design/installation of high temperature knife gate valves for bed ash drain to replace ball valves, saving $30K in annual repairs.
√ Analysis of high temperature vessel head cracking problem, location of design flaw, and implementation of design changes to save $15K in annual welding costs.

REVENUE GENERATION
√ Over $900K revenue for service and parts in 6 years.

TRAINING
√ 95% training success rate for both new and existing staff.

EDUCATION:
• BSET, Calhoon MEBA Engineering School
• Graduate Certificate, HVAC, Systems Design and Building Controls, Northeastern University

CERTIFICATIONS
DOE
• Pump Specialist (PSAT)
• Steam System Specialist
• Demand Side Management Specialist
ASSOCIATION OF FACILITIES ENGINEERING (AFE)
• Certified Plant Engineer (CPE)
OSHA
• 10 Hour Certification

LICENSING
• US Coast Guard license, Motor and Steam Vessels, Unlimited Horsepower, all endorsements including VSO, STCW,TWIC and Gas Turbines
• Commonwealth of Massachusetts certification, First Class Steam Engineer (Unlimited Horsepower)

I am eager to hear about opportunities for leading large field or marine engineering projects. Please feel free to contact me.

EXAMPLE #5:

 Summary

✦ PASSION FOR HOTEL INDUSTRY | TOP-NOTCH HOSPITALITY EXPERIENCE ✦

Since the start of my career in hospitality as a guest service agent, I have worked in every aspect of the industry – from catering & event management to sales, marketing, revenue, accounting & operations.

I'm known as a high-energy, decisive problem-solver with a zeal for creating well-considered, efficient operations. What makes me excel in my field:

HIGHLY ANALYTICAL, PENSIVE & DECISIVE MIND
✦ Conducted full-spectrum industry/financial analyses of businesses.
✦ Devised/implemented grand opening operations for 65,000 sq. ft. entertainment venue; created employee handbook, surveyed post-launch procedures, established sustainable business solutions.
✦ Spearheaded innovative marketing strategies to bolster sales for multi-property management firm.
✦ Adept at improving guest satisfaction and employee satisfaction scores.

WELL-ROUNDED BACKGROUND: PROFESSIONAL, ACADEMIC, TECHNICAL
✦ Professional experience in hotel, resort, and rental management. Consistently among the Top regional sellers for rental management firm.
✦ Graduate studies in economics, accounting, marketing research, quantitative analysis, business and finance. Ongoing professional development.
✦ Proficient in MS Office applications; experience with Delphi, Opera, Synxis, Easy RMS, Smith Travel Research, Epitome, Micros, and Fidelio.

SUPERIOR TIME MANAGEMENT
✦ Worked full-time while completing top-ranked MBA program for Hospitality in the U.S.
✦ Managed 100-person staff and planned dozens of weekly events while supervising all retail operations at busy entertainment complex.
✦ Handled reservations, supervised personnel, monitored customer service, and fielded inquiries for 2 high-traffic luxury hotel properties simultaneously.
✦ Department head of a AAA rated four diamond hotel.

Specialties:✦Hospitality | Hotels | Resorts | Tourism | Sales | Marketing Strategy | Events

✦Business Analysis & Development | Relationship Management | Accounting | Finance | Revenue Analysis & Management | Operations | Operational Forecasting

✦Employee Training | Policies & Procedures | Efficiency | Team Building

✦World Travel - I have visited: Dublin, Ireland | London, England | Florence, Rome & Naples, Italy | Paris & Aix en Provence, France | Montreal, Quebec City, Toronto, Canada

You are now half-way through your 18 steps to a KILLER LinkedIn® profile! Like us on Facebook[3] for more suggestions and to join a community of like-minded readers. Please share your comments . . . online!

---

3 How to Write a KILLER LinkedIn Profile Facebook Page - https://www.facebook.com/linkedinprofiletips

MISTAKE #8

No Descriptions or Weak Descriptions of Job Duties and Accomplishments

The Problem

People are looking at your LinkedIn profile to find out what you've done professionally. If you don't tell them, they might be left wondering what you are hiding, or whether you're just too lazy to write something. You are also losing out on opportunities to insert keywords into your profile, and your profile will not be 100% complete. What's the best approach to completing the Experience section on LinkedIn?

The Tune-Up

IMPORTANT: If you try to populate your LinkedIn profile by uploading your resume with the automated tool prompted by LinkedIn, you will end up with a mess. Don't do it!!! Similarly, do NOT use http://resume.linkedinlabs.com/ to create your resume from your LinkedIn profile. Its functionality is frustratingly limited.

For an effective Experience section, provide robust descriptions for your most recent and relevant jobs.

Note: You are not required to match your resume exactly to your LinkedIn profile. Since you have the option of *attaching* your resume to your profile **(see Mistake #14)**, you can use the Experience section on LinkedIn to complement rather than duplicate what's on the resume.

To edit your Experience section, while in Edit Profile mode, either click on your current position description next to your profile image (which will simply jump you down to your Experience section) or scroll down and find it.

Then click Add a position:

You can rearrange the entries within your Experience section by dragging and dropping the gray bar to the left of the entry.

Note that not all entries can be reordered. For instance, if you have 2 positions that are [date] to Present, you can rearrange them. If there is no gray bar, the item cannot be moved.

Should my Experience sections be copied from my resume?

I like to say that your LinkedIn Experience section should be completed as if you were talking to someone at a networking event. After all, LinkedIn is one big networking event! I generally prefer these sections to be written in the 1st person ("I") and to be fairly conversational, with some bullets of your accomplishments to make it clear what you're capable of achieving.

Don't forget that every section of LinkedIn is a repository for keywords! You can even put a Skills list in each of your Experience sections to beef up your search results. Sometimes, including a description of each company is an easy way to include keywords.

If you happen to be applying for a job using your LinkedIn profile, usually there is an option to attach a resume. If there is no such option, then it will be necessary for you to include all your resume bullets in your LinkedIn Experience.

For any resume-like bullets, start your phrases with verbs whenever possible (past tense verbs for past positions, present tense verbs for present positions). Rather than state your job duties, state what you accomplished or how you helped the organization you work(ed) for. The more concrete and quantifiable you are, the better (include keywords!) If you are struggling with how to write effective resume bullets, you might like my e-books, How to Write a WINNING Resume[1] and How to Write a STELLAR Executive Resume[2].

Some examples of great bullets are as follows:

- Secured record $5 million order from Varian Medical that was the largest single order taken in North America. Obtained trust of Management Team to implement key strategies for success.
- Improved team effectiveness by 25% in six months by redefining sales strategy and message, developing and documenting a formal sales process, and training the group in sales skills and use of new strategy.
- Teach 4 separate LinkedIn training courses
- LinkedIn 101: Learning the Basics of LinkedIn
- The Top Ten LinkedIn Business Development Strategies
- Sourcing and Recruiting Top Talent Using LinkedIn
- Tactical Research and Intelligence Gathering on LinkedIn

Note how these bullets leave you thinking, "It sounds like this person might be able to accomplish something for me."

Here's an example of a well-crafted LinkedIn Experience section, from The Essay Expert's client Ross Dabrow. Note that here, I break my own rule of using "I"; I break my own rules a lot!

---

1 How to Write a WINNING Resume . . . 50 Tips to Reach Your Job Search Target - http://www.amazon.com/gp/product/B00F05WFX0/

2 How to Write a STELLAR Executive Resume . . . 50 Tips to Reach Your Job Search Target
http://www.amazon.com/gp/product/B00F05W9I6/

Vice President Sales | Startup & Sales Growth Leadership |
Strategy Development | Change Management
T3Media (formerly Thought Equity Motion)
March 2013 – March 2014 (1 year 1 month)

Dates: 2013 to 2014; and 2006 to 2008 (3 Years)

► T3Media is an industry leader in digital content licensing and asset management.

Originally recruited in '06 by this industry startup to launch sales operations across 3 major U.S. media markets. Exerted strategic authority as VP of Sales, North America to achieve 112%+ YoY revenue growth and overtake top global market leaders in less than 2 years.

After expanding international business expertise for 5 years with other companies, received an exclusive invitation from T3Media's CEO and Head of Global Sales to return to the company, revive challenged Eastern sales division (Eastern U.S. and Canada) and restore market credibility.

► SUCCESS HIGHLIGHTS ◄

✓ Turned lowest-ranking region to highest company-wide performer within 1 year of turnaround by restructuring and leading sales organization to deliver 31% global licensing revenue.

✓ Improved monthly sales pipeline 27% via lead generation strategy.

✓ Slashed operating expenses 16% YoY by introducing efficiency controls across the region.

▾ 5 recommendations, including:

Nadine Blinn
Affiliate Manager at RealMatch, Inc.

Ross Dabrow is an excellent people manager who empowers, coaches and drives his team to success. He is a leader with keen... View↓

Matt Weiser
SVP, Global Sales & Sales Operations

Working with Ross is simply a pleasure. He is one of the most positive, upbeat people that I know, and his expertise in... View↓

Sometimes lackluster bullets or descriptions in your LinkedIn profile are an indication that your resume needs an overhaul as well. If you are a job seeker, consider hiring a professional resume writer to make sure that your entire presentation – resume and LinkedIn profile – are optimized to get you interviews! The Essay Expert offers resume writing services[3] for people at all stages of their careers and we would be happy to work with you.

Again, note that while you want your resume and LinkedIn profile to be consistent with each other, you might not want your LinkedIn profile to look *exactly* like your resume. To engage the reader in a more creative way, consider writing paragraphs instead of bullets on LinkedIn. If you are a job seeker, remember that many of the people reading your LinkedIn profile will have already seen your resume; if you are a previous user of LinkedIn applications, you can also link to the resume as discussed above through a Box.net link or a web link. You might want to give your viewers something a little different to read! Also, there might be items on your resume that are too confidential to share in the public space of LinkedIn. Rather than automatically copying your resume bullets into your LinkedIn profile, consider how you want to craft each section for your audience.

Results to Expect

Your readers will know what you've done at each of your jobs; they can learn more about you and determine whether you're someone they want to contact for further discussion.

---

3 The Essay Expert's Resume Writing Services - http://tinyurl.com/mwmanjm

Lack of Consistency/Discrepancies in Format and Structure —and Spelling, Grammar and Punctuation Errors

The Problem

Lack of consistency makes information harder to absorb because the reader starts to expect a particular format or grammatical construction—and instead gets something else. A mixed up format also appears unprofessional; people might think you did not take the time or know enough to put care into the details.

Spelling and grammatical errors will turn many of your readers off and absolutely do not project the professional image you want on LinkedIn. You can turn away employers, customers and clients with a single—and **avoidable** —error. Don't let this happen to you!

The Tune-Up

Be consistent. If you have a list of items that start with verbs, make them ALL start with verbs. If you are writing in the third person (e.g., *Ms. Bernstein is* an expert writer. *She holds* an English degree from Yale University . . .), write everything in the third person; if you're writing in the first person (e.g., *I teach* people how to use LinkedIn effectively; *I work* with job seekers and business owners), stick to the first person. If you use periods at the end of your bullets, do it everywhere. If you have a heading under one job description that says "Major Accomplishments," use the heading in all positions where you had major accomplishments.

Find a good editor to review your profile! Use your friends and family if they have skills in this area.

Another effective tool is Grammarly's extension for Chrome. Grammarly will tell you the number of "errors" it finds in your writing. This number will be in a red circle in the bottom right of the box you are working in.

To install Grammarly, open Chrome and visit http://tinyurl.com/grammarlyspellchecker. Then click the ADD TO CHROME button.

Unfortunately, the Grammarly extension is not yet available for other browsers, but here's the link to install Chrome if you'd like to try it out: https://www.google.com/chrome/.

Be careful! Grammarly often identifies as "errors" some things that constitute perfectly good English. The program is not a substitute for your own (or an editor's) discernment.

Results to Expect

Your consistency will demonstrate that you are organized, detail-oriented, and capable of clear communication. And your viewers will easily read your entire profile, all the way down to the Contact Settings. An error-free profile will have people saying, "Wow what a great profile! It's so well put together! This person presents himself/herself really well. I'm ready to take action."

MISTAKE #10

Unattractive Formatting

The Problem

Unattractive formatting looks unprofessional and it can make your profile hard to read. The most common formatting issue is with bullets. Does the following look attractive to you?

> • Directed $3 million dollar product division which developed solutions for FTSE 100 companies and others.
> • Successfully managed OEM technology relationships with HP, Lennox, Kyocera, Citzens and Brother.
> • Brought in new products and evaluated software development needs to maintain company's leading position in the technical world.

Even if your eyes don't hurt reading these bullets (mine do), you will probably notice that these tiny dots do not draw your attention to each statement. They are a weak formatting choice.

The Tune-Up

One of my favorite bullet formats to use on LinkedIn is the arrow: ▶
Look at the difference:

> ▶ Directed $3 million dollar product division which developed solutions for FTSE 100 companies and others.
> ▶ Successfully managed OEM technology relationships with HP, Lennox, Kyocera, Citzens and Brother.
> ▶ Brought in new products and evaluated software development needs to maintain company's leading position in the technical world.

Now my eyes are easily drawn to each of these notable achievements rather than straining to read them. (Unfortunately, hanging indents are still not an option on LinkedIn.)

Where can you find these symbols to insert into your profile? They do not always translate correctly from word processing programs, so feel free to copy and paste from my profile at http://www.linkedin.com/in/brendabernstein. You will also find lines and other symbols you might like. "Steal" away!

You might also like these bullets:

Symbol	Unicode (Arial Unicode MS)
▣	25A3
■	25A0
◈	25C8
✦	2726
▸	25B8

To use these bullets in your LinkedIn profile, insert a symbol into a Word document and copy and paste it into your LinkedIn profile. I've found that if you use Arial Unicode MS or Lucida Sans Unicode font, the symbols usually copy correctly.

If you want to experiment with different geometric shapes, or even letters in different languages, try copying and pasting your favorites from Wikipedia's List of Unicode characters[1] or (for foreign languages) use Google Translate.[2] Or, I recently found this site, where you can easily find, click and paste characters into your profile: http://copypastecharacter.com/all-characters.

You can also go to your character map. If you need to know how to access your character map, Google "character map for Mac" or "character map Windows7" (or Vista etc.), there are many sources that will help you find it. On a PC you can simply type "character" in the windows search bar and the character map will come up. Here's what it looks like:

---

1 Wikipedia: List of Unicode Characters - http://en.wikipedia.org/wiki/List_of_Unicode_characters

2 Google Translate - https://translate.google.com/

Next, simply choose the symbol you want to insert into your profile and double click on it. The symbol will appear in the "Characters to copy" box. You can double click on another character, and another, as many times as you want until you have the string of characters you want to insert:

Hit Copy (on the lower right) and then paste the characters into your profile.

If you are using a Mac, go to the Edit dropdown in your browser and choose Emoji & Symbols. You will then be able to click on the symbol you want and insert. Simple!

Want to see what some graphically designed profiles look like? See The Essay Expert's Sample LinkedIn Profiles.[3]

> **NOTE:** When you create a .pdf of your profile, these creative bullets appear as # signs. In my opinion, this slight glitch is worth it for the style it gives your on-line profile.

Here's another quick tip: The "pipe" (|) is a useful formatting tool. You can copy this character as well from my profile, or find the character on your keyboard (it's in different places on different keyboards, but is often on the same key as the backslash \ ). The pipe is most useful in your headline, e.g., Writing | Editing | Resumes | Cover Letters. It's clean and efficient.

Finally, here's how to insert a line across the page for emphasis (Note: lines take up 40 characters but I think they're worth it). The easiest way to create a line in your profile is to copy one from someone else's profile. Feel free to use mine!

View my profile on **Linked in**

Here's an example of a profile that utilizes this graphic successfully:

3 The Essay Expert's Sample LinkedIn Profiles - http://theessayexpert.com/samples/linkedin-profiles/

 Experience

Head of Creative, Director & Founding Partner (Tokyo - Japan)
SOUDESUNE K.K. | TOKYO

September 2009 – Present (5 years 2 months) | Shibuya, Tokyo, Japan

- ▶ Creative & Strategy Direction
- ▶ Brand Development - generate new ideas & concepts
- ▶ Driving the process of delivery
- ▶ Sourcing the components of successful delivery
- ▶ Communication with the mid- and top-brand management
- ▶ Brand Thinking for immediate pursuits with a solid foundation for the future
- ▶ Overseeing the process of brand creation, art and design delivery in the day to day operations
- ▶ Meeting / Liaising / Presenting to clients
- ▶ Acting as a strategic partner and assist client with creative strategy
- ▶ Create & Manage the creative brief process with clients
- ▶ Providing solutions that meet the client's brief and budget
- ▶ Negotiating with clients and internal teams about solutions across strategy, creative and execution related components

Brands & Clients: West | Davidoff | Algida | Pampers | Herbal Essence | Pringles | Iguaneye | Showa Gloves | P&G | Garde | Endymion | Quchy | Glance | Makers Revolution | 3M | Daito | Schwartzkopf | Shiseido | Eggworm | Elebrou | Wella | Toshiba | Fiat | Whisper | Vision Sound Museum

New Business Development / Managing Creative Director (Taipei - Taiwan)
Summit Group Taipei

February 2010 – December 2011 (1 year 11 months) | Taipei, Taiwan

Positioned as a Head of Design & Social Media Department
- ▶ New Business Development
- ▶ Creative Strategy
- ▶ Design Direction

Brands & Clients: Arma | SafeTouch | Clean & Protect | iFlyer | Eggworm

Results to Expect

Your profile will have a professional, clean and attractive look. People will enjoy looking at it. When I changed my profile format, I got an email complimenting me on the new look. That's the kind of result you want.

MISTAKE #11

Blank Specialties and/or Skills Sections

The Specialties section no longer exists for new members or those who did not populate it when they had the chance. For seasoned members, Specialties still exists *within* the Background / Summary section. You will see it once you click on your Summary section.

Summary

▶ Do you struggle with writing about yourself? Stop trying to do it alone!

We work intensively and personally with job seekers, college/MBA applicants and companies to create powerfully written resumes, application essays, LinkedIn profiles and marketing content.

If you have a writing project that's not getting done or not getting the results you want, whether it is...

You will then see the following screen:

Summary

Summary

best-selling author of How to Write a KILLER LinkedIn Profile.

▶ College / MBA Application Essays
Applying to college or business school? You need essays that "pop"! We coach you to write application essays that give you the best possible chance of acceptance into the school of your choice.

▶ Business Writing - B2B & B2C
If your company is growing, you need written materials to support it. The Essay Expert will ensure you present a professional image that lands you new clients and deals.

Clients report unprecedented results from working with The Essay Expert. Contact us now ... because you need to "look good on paper."

Specialties

Resumes | Executive Resumes | Cover Letters | Professional Bios | LinkedIn Profiles | LinkedIn Training | College Essays | College Admissions | College Applications | MBA Admissions Consulting | EMBA Admissions Consulting | Personal Statements | Scholarship Applications | B2B & B2C Business Writing | Web Copy | Proposals | Reports | Brochures

To help streamline how your profile is displayed, we've combined specialties with the Summary section. You can add these specialties to your Summary, but you'll need to edit the section so everything fits. Append specialties to summary

Note the suggestion at the bottom of this box to "Append specialties to summary." I do not recommend that you do this! If you do, you will lose out on 500 characters' worth of keywords or have to cut down your Summary section; and once you delete your Specialties section you won't be able to add it back!

For new users who don't have a Specialties section, no worries. You get to use the Skills & Endorsements section.

The Problem

If you have a Specialties section (not everyone does, as explained above), then both the Specialties and Skills sections are important areas in which to list your keywords. Whether or not you have a Specialties section, the Skills & Endorsements section is your best opportunity to appear in recruiters' searches conducted for people with your skills. The Specialties section gets searched when people do an Advanced Search.

If you do not complete these two sections (or at least the Skills section), you will lose a lot of leverage in LinkedIn searches. You also will not be able to get Endorsements if you do not have a Skills & Endorsements section. Endorsements can be used by potential clients, employers and recruiters to confirm that you have the skills you claim to have!

The Tune-Up

Make a list of your areas of expertise, and keep them short and to the point – the majority of these items should be keywords people might search for on LinkedIn. List them in Specialties and in Skills & Endorsements, and make sure this content is distinct from the content in the Summary section.

Here's a sample of what a Specialties section can look like (this person is a specialist in LinkedIn):

> Specialties: LinkedIn Lead Generation, LinkedIn Marketing, LinkedIn Expert Positioning, LinkedIn Seminars, LinkedIn Coaching, LinkedIn Training, LinkedIn Counseling, LinkedIn Ebook, LinkedIn Online Training, LinkedIn Profile Checklist, LinkedIn Consulting, LinkedIn Advice, LinkedIn Keynote Speaker, LinkedIn Trainer, LinkedIn Career Development

And here is a sample Skills & Endorsements section:

Skills & Endorsements

Top Skills

99+	Resume Writing
31	Executive Resumes
20	C-Level Resumes
60	LinkedIn Profiles
90	LinkedIn
49	Professional Bios
21	College Application...
19	MBA Admissions...
94	Cover Letters

If someone searches for "Security Clearance" using the Advanced Search function, something like this will appear:

Although the initial list that appears is focused on *jobs* related to Security Clearance, you can click on "People" to get a list of people who have the keyword Security Clearance in their profile. Don't you want to appear on lists like this for your target keywords?

Don't have a Skills section? Or don't know how to manage it?

To add the Skills section, go to your Profile and look just below the top portion. You will see a list of sections Recommended for you. Chances are if you don't have a Skills & Endorsements section, LinkedIn will recommend that you add one!

Once you have added the section, you will be able to add and remove skills and manage your endorsements for those skills. In Edit Profile view, scroll down to your Skills section and click on the Add skill button:

Skills & Endorsements   + Add skill   ↕

If this is your first time using the Skills section, you will see this:

Skills & Endorsements   + Add skill   ↕

Skills and Endorsements Settings ②

I want to be endorsed ⦿ Yes ○ No

☐ Include me in endorsement suggestions to my connections

☐ Show me suggestions to endorse my connections

☑ Send me notifications via email when my connections endorse me

Add & Remove ② | Manage Endorsements ②

What are your areas of expertise?   Add

←⬚→ Drag to reorder.

Save   Cancel

You will have the option to allow LinkedIn to suggest endorsements for you to your connections, see endorsement suggestions from your connections, and/or receive email notifications when connections endorse you.

To add skills, begin typing your desired skill and you will be given a list to choose from; whenever possible, choose skills that auto-populate, since these are the skills most searched for, especially by recruiters. However, you do not need to stick to the list. You can add up to 50 skills.

Add & Remove ② | Manage Endorsements ②

project   Add

Project+

Project **Management**   0   C-Level Resumes ✕

Project **Planning**   sional Bios ✕

Microsoft Project   Consulting ✕

Software Project **Management**   ✕ 🔲 Public Speaking ✕

Once your Skills section is established, it will look more like this:

Skills and Endorsements Settings ⊘

I want to be endorsed | ◉ Yes ○ No

☐ Include me in endorsement suggestions to my connections
☐ Show me suggestions to endorse my connections
☑ Send me notifications via email when my connections endorse me

Add & Remove ⊘ | Manage Endorsements ⊘

What are your areas of expertise? [Add]
You can still add: 10

As of April 2014, you can rearrange your skills by dragging and dropping the boxes so that your most pertinent skills are located at the top of the list. Save to complete your changes.

You can remove a skill by simply clicking the X next to its name.

You might find yourself getting emails telling you that someone wants to endorse your for "new" Skills not currently listed on your profile. This might sound like a great idea, but remember that there was probably a reason you didn't list that skill in your profile in the first place—either you don't have that skill, or you don't want to market it.

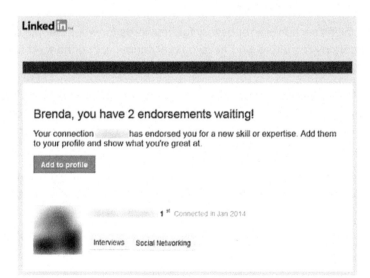

In this situation, I would recommend resisting the urge to click the Add to profile button. In addition, when you log into your profile, press Skip to decline adding the Skills.

There are other ways you can take control over your Skills section. One of them is to fill in ALL 50 Skills. With no room to add new skills, there will be less likelihood of inappropriate ones being added to your profile, because it would require you to delete one of your skills before you could add the new one.

The Skills listed at the top of your list are the ones with the most endorsements, so ask connections to endorse you for the Skills you want to appear at the top.

To show or hide your endorsements, click on Manage Endorsements at the top the grey area. You will see a list of all of the contacts who have endorsed you for that particular skill. You then have the option to show or hide either all of your endorsements or individual endorsements.

A common question I am asked by long-time LinkedIn members who still have a Specialties section is: "Do I need to complete both the Specialties AND the Skills sections?" The answer is "Yes, if you have that option." For as long as both sections exist, complete them both!

Why? Because the Specialties section is a repository for keywords for when people do an Advanced Search. And the Skills is searchable by recruiters who have paid accounts with enhanced functionality. You want to rank highly in both types of searches.

According to LinkedIn, "Accumulating a high number of endorsements for a skill adds credibility to your profile, and shows that your professional network recognizes you have that skill," as well as "contributes to the strength of [your] profile, and increases the likelihood [you'll] be discovered for opportunities related to the skills [your] connections know [you] possess."

For an article about some of the frustrating aspects of the Skills section, including getting endorsed for skills you don't have and by people who are not truly familiar with your skills, see my blog post, 4 Ways to Take Control of Your LinkedIn Endorsements.[1]

If you're not getting as many endorsements as you'd like, try endorsing other people! You might be amazed at how quickly they return the favor.

Results to Expect

According to Link Humans, "members who include skills get around 13 times more profile views." Furthermore, people will understand better where your skills lie; they will endorse you, giving you more credibility; and they will "find" you when they search on your chosen keywords and skills.

---

1 4 Ways to Take Control of Your LinkedIn Endorsements - http://tinyurl.com/p5t7a2r

The more endorsements you have as a job seeker, the more likely you are to be contacted by a recruiter with a premium account.

More endorsements and more traffic to your profile mean more opportunities for you!

There's a great article from the LinkedIn Blog about Endorsements[2] that provides some great advice about giving and receiving endorsements. I recommend that you read it!

2 Endorse and Be Endorsed - http://blog.linkedin.com/2012/12/18/endorse-and-be-endorsed/

MISTAKE #12

Not Sharing LinkedIn Activity Updates and Other Valuable Information

The Activity Update bar can be found on your homepage; it is a place for you to report on your current goings on. You might be familiar with this type of function if you spend time on Twitter or Facebook. Here's what it looks like:

66 Share an update   Upload a presentation   Publish a post

What's on your mind?

Share with: Public   Share

The Problem

This feature is your opportunity to let your readers know that you're active in your life and in your field. If you do not use this function, your name and updates will not appear in the ongoing activity feed found on your connections' homepages.

The Tune-Up

Keep your Updates current and share valuable information consistently. There are many tools available to help you collect and curate great information for sharing. Here are just a few:

- **Pocket**[1]: Save articles, blog posts, videos and images for later use.
- **Feedly**[2]: Follow blogs, podcasts, YouTube channels and publications, and access the content anytime.
- **Google Alerts**[3]: Get email notifications when Google finds new results on a topic that interests you.
- **Listly**[4]: Create lists of just about anything and let people contribute.

You can include photos or presentations with your updates. Simply click the Upload a presentation tab and choose a photo or presentation from your files.

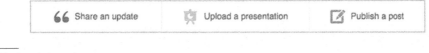

---

1 Pocket - https://getpocket.com/

2 Feedly - https://feedly.com/

3 Google Alerts - https://www.google.com/alerts

4 Listly - http://list.ly/

This is what your post will look like when you share an image:

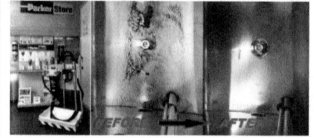

If you want to view your activity updates by hovering over your Profile tab and clicking on Your Updates.

You can also view other members' activity updates by clicking the down arrow next to their Send a message or Send [name] InMail button and then choosing View recent activity:

Once you know what information you want to share, you have many ways to do so. Six good options are highlighted below:

Option #1: HootSuite

HootSuite.com allows you to send updates to Twitter, Facebook and LinkedIn all with one click. You can simply post the update you want to HootSuite and schedule it to post to the social media site you choose at the time you choose. Or if you have your own blog or a favorite blog by someone else, you can send an RSS feed (a stream that contains each of the articles as it is posted) to the social media account(s) of your choosing. That way your blog posts can automatically post to your LinkedIn Activity Update bar.

Here's how to share your blog:

After logging in to HootSuite, hover over the launch bar on the left side of your account. Click on Settings >
RSS/Atom:

Click the + sign to add a new feed. You might need to upgrade to a paid account ($5.99/month) to use this
feature.

Paste your feed URL in the field provided. Then select the social sites you would like the feed to post to.

Add an RSS/Atom Feed   ✕

Feed URL

http://yoursite.com/feed

Network to send feed items to:

👤

👤 BrendaBernstein   🐦 ▲

👤 TheEssayExpert   🐦 ≡

👤 Brenda Bernstein   ☆ 📘

🔲 How to Write a Killer LinkedIn P...   ↪

   The Essay Expert   ✈

   Brenda Bernstein, Owner, The E...   in

📊 Business Connections of Greater...   in ▼

Clear | ➕   Show all ▾

~~Example: New Blog Post or News Update.~~

URL shortener for links:

ow.ly   ▾

Cancel   Save Feed

Edit any other preferred options and Save Feed.

For posting WordPress blogs to your LinkedIn profile or other social media accounts, you can also use the *Publicize* function from the JetPack Plugin[5].

Option #2: Activity Updates

Access your Update bar from the Home tab. Write something current—about what you're learning, a project you're working on, even your latest favorite quotation. Show us you're alive! You might even choose to reveal your sense of humor (keep it clean folks!) Some clients have had success posting that they are seeking to relocate to a particular city—it is possible to catch the attention of recruiters that way.

If you blog once/week this solution might be the best one for you. You then have the option of sharing the update on LinkedIn and Twitter.

Homepage image:

❝❝ Share an update   📊 Upload a presentation   ✍ Publish a post

What's on your mind?   ⚙

---

5 JetPack Plugin - http://jetpack.me/support/publicize/linkedin/

If there is an update you wish to share with only your 1st tier connections on LinkedIn, select Share with: Just your connections from the drop down:

Want to know the effectiveness of your postings? From your homepage, see at a glance how many people have viewed, liked and commented on your latest update.

Brenda Bernstein
Essay & Resume Writer ★ Executive Resu…

Improve your profile

22 people viewed your profile in the past 3 days

136 views on your update "31 ways to make the holiday season work f…"

Option #3: Long-Form Posts

According to LinkedIn's Official Blog post, The Definitive Professional Publishing Platform:[6]

> "When a member publishes a [long-form] post on LinkedIn, their original content becomes part of their professional profile, is shared with their trusted network and [can] reach the largest group of professionals ever assembled. Now members have the ability to follow other members that are not in their network and build their own group of followers."

LinkedIn's total publishing platform includes: 1) sharing updates via your homepage and 2) publishing long-form posts, or articles. Both are accessed from the same place on your homepage. Perhaps the coolest thing about these long-form posts is that they are searchable *outside* of LinkedIn. That means readers don't even need to have a LinkedIn account in order to view your work. Think of the reach you can have!

Are you concerned about copyright on the articles you publish on LinkedIn? Here's a message from LinkedIn regarding published content:

> At LinkedIn, we want to help you make the most of your professional life. Part of that is showing the world more about who you are and what you know by sharing ideas, starting conversations, and inspiring others with your work.

> So, that raises a question: who owns all of the content you post on LinkedIn? You do, and you always have. We've updated our User Agreement[7] (effective October 23, 2014) to reinforce our commitment to respecting what's yours. Whether it's an update, photo, comment, post, presentation, portfolio, or anything else, we want to make it clear that you're in control of your content.

6 The Definitive Professional Publishing Platform - http://tinyurl.com/pkyryx2

7 LinkedIn User Agreement - https://www.linkedin.com/legal/preview/user-agreement

Here are some highlights (you can read more in our blog post)[8]:

- You're in the driver's seat. We'll always ask your permission before using your content in third-party ads, publications, or websites. We've always done this, but now our User Agreement specifically spells it out.

- You decide when your content goes. If you delete something from our platform, we won't use it anymore.

- Share wherever or whenever you'd like. We don't own or have exclusive rights to your content. It's yours, so feel free to repost it anywhere, however you want.

Thanks for being a member! The LinkedIn Team

As of January 2015, all members of English-speaking countries have the ability to publish long-form post; shortly thereafter, LinkedIn will be expanding that privilege to all of the languages they support.

To create a long-form post once you are given Publishing rights, go to your homepage and click on Publish a post:

You will arrive at the Create a New Post page. To publish an article, simply add your content, along with images and pertinent links.

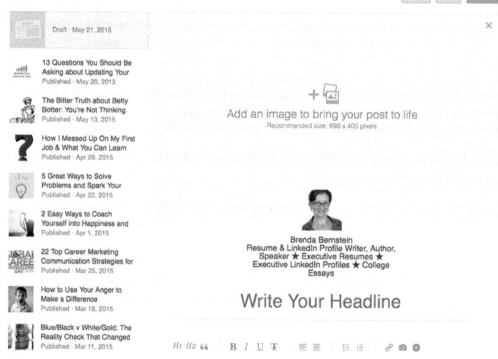

Over 40,000 long-form posts are published every week. According to a study by OkDork and Search Wilderness[9], the most successful posts followed these guidelines:

- **Keep your title short and sweet.** Title with more than 40-49 characters can get cut off.
- **Make it visual.** Posts with at least 8 images perform 2.4 times better.
- **Don't use videos and other multimedia!** This might be surprising, but fewer people view articles that include videos (as opposed to static images, which boost views).
- **Keep it clear.** Include subheadings—ideally 5 of them—so your article is easy to read.
- **Maintain a reasonable length.** Articles between 1900 and 2000 words are read more often.
- **Go neutral.** Posts that were neither positive or negative ranked higher.
- **Simplify.** Articles that met the reading level of an 11-year-old ranked better.
- **Get Likes.** The more Likes you have, the more views you will get.
- **Publish on Thursdays.** Thursday posts get the most views.
- **Don't pose your title as a question.** Titles that contained a question didn't fare as well.

Always proofread and preview your article before publishing! Once you click Publish, your post is shared.

Here's what people in your network will see in their inbox when you post an article:

9 10 Data-Driven Steps to Dominate LinkedIn Publishing - http://tinyurl.com/k2e3dw2

Here is what your post will look like on the homepage of your connections:

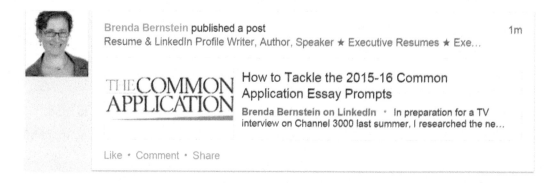

Each time someone likes or comments on your post, it is brought to the top of the page again.

Your posts will also appear in the Posts section of your profile, just beneath your photo. And they can be searched via the Posts option from the search bar drop down:

Interested readers can click through to the post page where they can then follow you and comment on your article, even if they are not currently in your network. Social media statistics and share buttons above your post allow readers to spread your work beyond LinkedIn!

Be sure to utilize keywords in your posts. LinkedIn uses a special algorithm to tag long-form posts into categories called "channels" and to suggest posts for its members. If your article is tagged, it will appear to LinkedIn members with the most relevant profile content. So do some keyword research for your field, or hire someone to do it for you, and build your posts using SEO practices!

Remember to use the "add tags" feature that appears below your article. Inserting relevant keywords here will help your article get found.

Published and draft posts are listed in the right sidebar of your Create a New Post page.

Your Posts

Draft · Apr 1, 2015

22 Top Career Marketing Communication Strategies for
Published · Mar 25, 2015

How to Use Your Anger to Make a Difference
Published · Mar 18, 2015

Blue/Black v White/Gold: The Reality Check That Changed
Published · Mar 11, 2015

Losada Colada: The Power of Positive Thought and Action
Published · Feb 18, 2015

A Fool-Proof Way to Achieve Any Goal – And That's a
Published · Feb 18, 2015

Overused LinkedIn Buzzwords of 2014 ... At Long Last!!
Published · Jan 28, 2015

You can view all of your published posts from your profile, listed in the "Posts" section.

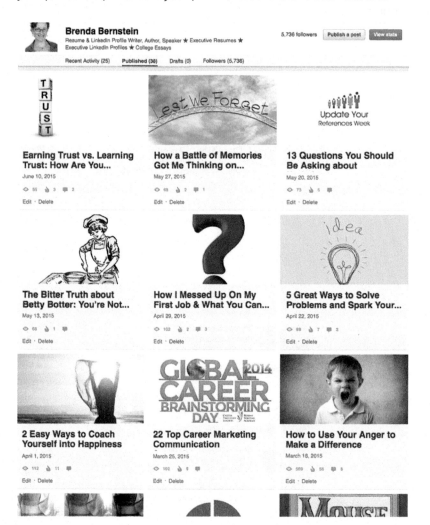

You can also view them from your publishing dashboard, where you can measure each article's success by reviewing its stats. To find your dashboard, go to your profile, hover over the down arrow to the right of your View profile as button and select View recent activity.

Then click on Published.

Note that the number of followers you have is equal to your 1st tier connections plus unconnected followers.

When you have your Notifications summary turned on in Settings (Privacy & Settings > Communications > Set the frequency of emails), you will also receive status updates on your posts:

Brenda, see how your posts are doing as of Sunday, June 14, 2015 11:59 PM PDT	View your stats		
Recent posts	Page views	Likes	Comments
Earning Trust vs. Learning Trust: How Are You Doing? Jun 10, 2015	70	4	2
How a Battle of Memories Got Me Thinking on Memorial Day May 27, 2015	68	2	1
13 Questions You Should Be Asking about Updating Your References May 20, 2015	74	5	--
The Bitter Truth about Betty Botter: You're Not Thinking Straight May 13, 2015	66	1	--
How I Messed Up On My First Job & What You Can Learn From My Mistakes! Apr 29, 2015	103	2	3
5 Great Ways to Solve Problems and Spark Your Creativity Apr 22, 2015	89	7	2
2 Easy Ways to Coach Yourself into Happiness and Success Apr 1, 2015	112	11	--

As with activity updates, you have the option to tweet your long-form post.

For LinkedIn's tips and best practices for publishing long-form posts, visit LinkedIn's Help Center topic Long-Form Posts on LinkedIn Overview.[10]

Have you utilized LinkedIn's long-form post feature? If so, what benefits have you enjoyed? And if not, what are you waiting for?

Option #4: Sharing Bookmarklet

LinkedIn's Sharing Bookmarklet allows you to share anything from your web browser straight into your LinkedIn Activity Updates (or to groups or individuals on LinkedIn)!

If you're on a desktop or laptop, access this feature at https://www.linkedin.com/static?key=browser_bookmarklet. From the top tabs, find Sharing Bookmarklet, and click the Change Browser drop down menu:

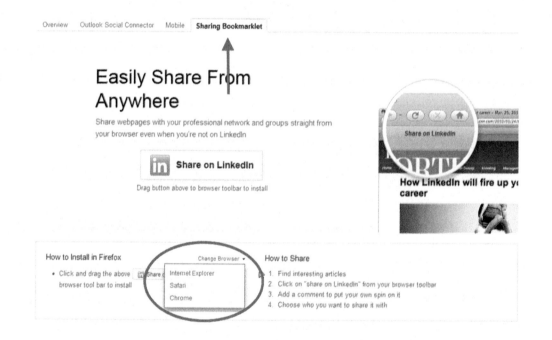

Open the relevant browser, then follow the installation instructions (they are different for each browser). Once installed, you will be able to share any web page on LinkedIn! Here's an example:

10 Long-Form Posts on LinkedIn - Overview - https://help.linkedin.com/app/answers/detail/a_id/47445/ft/eng

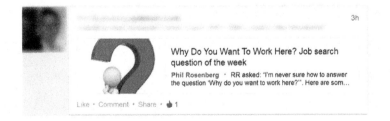

You may choose to share your update with groups or individuals who would be interested in the article, page or event you want to publicize.

To use the bookmarklet:

1. From the web page you want to share, click in the browser bar and start typing "Share news on LinkedIn . . . "

2. You should then see the bookmark listed with a star.

3. Click the bookmark and the sharing window should open up, populated and ready to go!

Option #5: Share Across LinkedIn

Share other people's updates from the items that appear on your homepage. To do this, look at the bottom of the update you wish to share and click on Share.

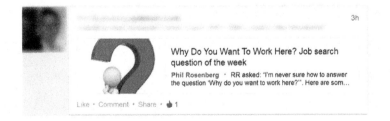

You will have the option to share with everyone (Public) or just your network (Connections). You can also share with individuals and include a personalized message simultaneously.

Good items for anyone to share in Activity Updates are favorite inspirational quotations. You can also announce your accomplishments, certifications, and important life events. If you are a business owner or conference promoter marketing an event, use this opportunity to let people know about it! And if you are announcing an event or discussing a topic that is selective, invite an exclusive crowd by clicking on Send to individuals. Then write them an enticing note:

Click Share and spread the word to the world! The more connections you have or the more people you share with, the more people will see your post and possibly share it with their connections as well.

Give Credit Where Credit is Due

LinkedIn's Mentions feature is a great little tool for crediting connections in your updates. If you type the "@" symbol, followed by the name of a connection or a company in your Update box or a comment field on the Homepage, the field will auto-generate potential people or companies you can mention. (For more information, see this LinkedIn help article, Mention People and Companies in Your Updates—Frequently Asked Questions.[11])

Select the connection you want from the drop-down, write your post and click the Share button. The person or company you mentioned will automatically be notified that they have been mentioned.

In addition to first-degree connections, you can also mention other LinkedIn members engaged in conversations in the comment sections of posts on the LinkedIn Homepage. Mentions make it easier for you to start conversations with your network while also enabling you to respond in real time when someone begins a conversation with you.

Option #6: Comment and Like

Stay active on LinkedIn. When you add a connection, add or comment on a group discussion, post a job, or even just like another Update, it will go into LinkedIn's news feed and show up on your connections' homepages.

---

11 Mention People and Companies in Your Updates - Frequently Asked Questions
https://help.linkedin.com/app/answers/detail/a_id/34936

You will also be able to view a full list of your recent activity and that of others via their profile page. Click View recent activity:

To make sure your activity history is viewable go to your Privacy & Settings and click on Select who can see your activity feed:

You'll then have the option to choose between only you, everyone, your network or just your connections. Everyone has different considerations when choosing how public to be with their profile, so choose the option that meets your needs and goals.

Results to Expect

The more you post updates and share them, and the more you use the @Mention feature, the more your activity will be publicized and the more you will stay top of mind with your connections.

Publishing long-form posts will generate a wide audience and could turn you into a "top influencer" on LinkedIn if your posts are popular enough.

LinkedIn reaches more followers per post (20%) than Facebook (2%) or Twitter (4%)! So be sure to put this tool to good use.

Linked in™

Brenda, see how your posts are doing
as of Sunday, August 10, 2014 11:59 PM PDT

See your posts

Recent posts	Page views	Likes	Comments
Job Search Strategy: Get 3 Offers Jul 29, 2014	349	4	4
Think Personal Development is Optional? Think Again Jul 24, 2014	131	2	--
How to Publish Long-Form Posts on LinkedIn Jul 22, 2014	323	6	3
Are You Self-Critical? I Sure Am. Jul 17, 2014	778	29	5
The #1 Way to Solve Business Disputes Jul 15, 2014	1,728	65	7

According to LinkedIn's Official Blog[12], "When a LinkedIn member shares six pieces of content, on average, they receive six profile views and make two new connections, which helps them strengthen their professional brands. At the same time, the company they work for receives six job views, three Company Page views, and one Company Page follower, which helps them better hire, market, and sell."

Every time you post original content, you establish yourself further as a thought leader in your field. Experts deemed worthy by LinkedIn (the top 150 most influential contributors) are featured in LinkedIn's Pulse[13], where top contributors' profiles and recent posts are shared with the world!

If my own experience is any indication, the more active you are in sharing information, the more you will be noticed by potential clients and employers; many of the people who read and engage with your offerings will remember you and tell their connections about you. In a business world where networking is king, you can't ask for better than that.

---

12 Introducing LinkedIn Elevate: Helping Companies Empower Their Employees To Share Content
http://blog.linkedin.com/2015/04/13/elevate/

13 LinkedIn® Pulse - https://www.linkedin.com/pulse/

Special Sections not Utilized

The Problem

Special Sections: LinkedIn frequently adds new sections appropriate for special groups like artists and students, for activities like volunteerism, and for skills like languages. You might fall into one of these categories and be at a disadvantage to the artist who completed a portfolio; the student who completed the student section; or the volunteer with a robust Volunteering & Causes section.

Furthermore, you might be at a loss when attempting to include all the aspects of who you are into your profile unless you utilize some of these special sections.

The Tune-Up

These sections allow you to present information in an organized fashion so you don't have to get everything across in your Summary or Experience sections. If you are an artist, use the Portfolio section. If you have taken courses you want to report, check out the Courses section. Speak languages? Try Languages. Volunteer? Complete the Volunteering & Causes section (you don't have to fit it all into the Experience section). Other sections include Projects, Honors & Awards, Organizations, Test Scores, Certifications and Patents. You can even post your blog under your Publications section; just add a live URL that links directly to your blog for anyone who wants to take a look!

See the next page to see what some of the special sections look like:

 Publications

How to Write a KILLER LinkedIn Profile

Self-Published. #1 Top-Rated in Amazon's Business Writing Category

February 2012

Read this Best-Selling E-Book and Tune Up your LinkedIn Profile!

Are you getting the results that you want from your LinkedIn profile? If not, this book is for you. I provide you with 18 detailed strategies and writing tips that other "LinkedIn experts" don't cover. First I tell you how to get found on LinkedIn, and then I tell you how to keep people reading.

By following the advice in this... **more**

The Essay Expert Blog | Resumes | LinkedIn | Personal Statements

Brenda Bernstein | The Essay Expert LLC

March 2009

Weekly wisdom on resume, LinkedIn, personal statement and other writing topics from Brenda Bernstein, The Essay Expert!

How to Write a WINNING Resume: 50 Tips to Reach Your Job Search Target

The Essay Expert

September 2013

If you're eager to read a do-it-yourself resume guide that's easy-to-read, practical and up-to-date, this is the book you've been looking for! How to Write a WINNING Resume takes you through the resume writing process step by step, from thinking through your approach to creating a great format, crafting effective branding statements and bullets, and handling specific challenges.

 Honors & Awards

TORI Award Winner, Best New Graduate Resume, 3rd Place

Career Directors International

October 2012

Each year, CDI hosts the resume writing industry's most prestigious Toast of the Resume Industry™ (TORI) resume writing competition. This is an international competition in which contestants submit their best work in a category.

TORI Award Nominee, Best Re-Entry Resume

Career Directors International

September 2012

TORI Award Nominee, Best Creative Resume

Career Directors International

September 2011

To add a section, simply click on Profile from the main menu:

Once in edit mode, you will see a list of sections LinkedIn has recommended for you just below the upper portion of your profile. Click the desired section to add it to your profile.

Add a section to your profile – be discovered for your next career step.

Language
This can help you find a new job, get a promotion, or transfer overseas.

Add language

Organizations
Add more color to your professional identity to show who you are.

Add organizations

Honors & Awards
Show the recognition you've earned.

Add honors & awards

Test Scores
Here's another way to show your accomplishments.

Add test scores

Courses
Showing more information about your background will help you get found for more opportunities.

Add courses

Patents
Showcase your innovation and expertise.

Add patents

Projects
This helps show your skills, experience, and people you've worked with.

Add projects

Publications
Publications are a great way to show off your professional accomplishments.

Add publications

Certifications
Members with a certification on their profile get double the profile views.

Add certifications

Advice for Contacting
Make sure you're found for the opportunities you're interested in.

Add advice for contacting

LinkedIn will automatically jump down to the place in your profile where the new section will appear (you can always move it later) and you can begin adding your information.

Projects

Name *

Occupation
Choose...   ▼

Date Switch to date range
Month...   ▼   Year...   ▼

Project URL

Team Member(s) *

👤 Brenda Bernstein   + Add team member

Drag to reorder contributors

Description

Save   Cancel

Add project

Save and presto!

You can get creative with what you list where. For instance, list your blog as a publication and include the link, allowing people to click directly to the blog. Or list details of projects in the Projects section that you don't have room to explain in your Summary or Experience sections. LinkedIn's multitude of section choices provides quite a bit of room for experimentation!

The order of Certifications, Honors & Awards, and other sections can easily be rearranged, and the entries within each section can sometimes be reordered. Some entries, however, are ordered the way LinkedIn says they should be ordered! To rearrange the entries within special sections, drag and drop the gray bar to the left of the entry:

See Bonus Tip #6 for tips on reordering your profile sections.

Results to Expect

You will be able to share much more information than is possible without these special sections; and you can organize it in a way that brings attention to important aspects of your career and education. No longer will you struggle with how to share about your volunteerism, impressive courses or accomplishments. It's all laid out neatly for you!

MISTAKE #14

No Portfolio Items in your Summary and Experience Sections

LinkedIn used to provide a full palette of "Partner Applications" to its members. Some of the more popular were Events (for promoting webinars and other events), Box.net (for attaching files), and SlideShare (where you could embed a presentation or video). LinkedIn has replaced some of these apps with a Portfolio function that allows users to add links to images, presentations, videos, and documents to their profiles.

The Problem

If you don't use LinkedIn's Portfolio function, your profile will be one-dimensional (*i.e.,* boring) and you will miss out on accessible, free marketing for yourself and your business.

The Tune-Up

In your Summary and Experience sections, you can add files or links to videos, images, documents or presentations by clicking on the box with a + sign in the corner.

Summary

Click to add a video, image, document, presentation...

You will then see the following:

Add to Summary:

http://

Supported Providers

or   Upload a file

Continue   Cancel

The possibilities are endless of what you can link to or upload here. If you choose Upload File you will be brought to your computer's document files.

Once you upload a file, you can move it to other sections of your profile by clicking on that item.

∨ SEE MORE ∨

Then go to Move this media to and choose the section you want to move it to:

Title *

Brenda Bernstein LinkedIn Resume

Description

Every resume writer needs a resume, right? Click here to view mine.

Move this media to

~~Summary~~

[Save] [Cancel] Remove this media

Following are some ideas of material you can use to populate the Portfolio function on your LinkedIn profile; some of these ideas come from the days of Partner Applications!

I. EVENTS

If you are promoting an event, attach the link so you can include an event image right in your Summary or Experience section.

II. DOCUMENTS, INCLUDING YOUR RESUME

Here's what my multi-media portfolio looks like with a resume uploaded directly to the profile:

Video of Testimonials for The Essay Expert   LinkedIn and Resume Webinar & Events S…

Brenda Bernstein's Amaz…   Brenda Bernstein LinkedI…   LinkedIn®'s Hidden Secr…

˅ SEE MORE ˅

Note: If you choose post your resume to LinkedIn, you may want to remove your address from the header. Assuming you have a public profile, your resume, along with the information on it, will be available to the public. Of course it will also be available to hackers if they break into LinkedIn, which we know is a real possibility from the events of June 6, 2012 (when multiple LinkedIn profiles were hacked).

What do you want to share with your LinkedIn audience? You can build your image through adding links to any important documents and web pages. Have fun!

III. SLIDESHARE

[Note that the following instructions are current as of August 2015 and new features are being added.][1]

You can log in to SlideShare with your LinkedIn username and password and import your LinkedIn profile information to complete your SlideShare profile. With a single click, you can follow all your LinkedIn contacts

---

1 SlideShare Is Rebranding to LinkedIn SlideShare - http://tinyurl.com/nknoa94

through SlideShare, thus ensuring that you receive notifications of their updated content and comments. You can also announce your SlideShare uploads to your connections.

When you are logged into both your SlideShare and LinkedIn accounts and you upload a new presentation, document or video to SlideShare with your status set to Public, it will *automatically* append it as a file associated with your LinkedIn Summary. This is a great feature; be aware, however, that adding content to your profile this way will not generate an activity update.

To get your new presentation to show up as an update in all of your connections' homepage feeds, upload your files to SlideShare before you log into LinkedIn, then add the content to your Summary by adding a Link. Be sure you have turned on your activity broadcasts in Privacy & Settings first (see the introduction to Section 2 for how to do this).

To post the link to a SlideShare presentation to your Summary or Experience sections, start by clicking on the box with the **+** sign:

How do you get the correct link for your presentation? In SlideShare, go to your list of presentations by hovering over your profile image and clicking My uploads:

Hovering over the image of your presentation will reveal a pop-up button to add that presentation to your profile.

When you upload new presentations, you will see the option to share and add them to your profile right away:

Alternatively, you can click on one of the images and you will be brought to the page with the presentation:

Copy the URL for that page and paste it into the box on LinkedIn. LinkedIn will pull the title and description from SlideShare. Then click the Add to profile button.

Title *

LinkedIn®'s Hidden Secrets Revealed!   ×

Description

Find out some of LinkedIn's lesser-known tips and tricks for job seekers and company owners!

Add to profile   Cancel

The presentation or video will then be part of your permanent LinkedIn profile until you decide to remove or change it, plus your connection will be notified via their homepage feed that you have added it! The post will look something like this:

Brenda Bernstein has an updated professional gallery.

Brenda Bernstein Is
On The Sales
Whisperer® Podcast

The Sales Whisperer Podcast Interview With LinkedIn Expert Brenda...

thesaleswhisperer.com · About Today's Guest: Brenda Bernstein was an English major at Yale before obtaining law degree, but she was always a writer. Her friends would always ask her for help on resumes, job applications, etc. After college she began...

Like · Comment · 18s ago

In October 2014, Slideshare created a tool called Professional Journey.[2] This is a fun application that takes your current LinkedIn Recommendations, Education, Experience and Skills sections and creates a brief presentation.

When you first access Professional Journey, you'll be given the option to expand your network. I recommend checking all of these options with the exception of "Display my SlideShare uploads on LinkedIn.com." This option will post any presentation to your connections' homepages as soon as you hit Publish. This can be embarrassing if you have made an error. It's always best to review your published work prior to sharing.

Expand your network!

☑ **Follow my LinkedIn contacts on SlideShare**
  Get updates when they post to SlideShare

☑ **Follow Slideshare company page on LinkedIn.com**
  So you will find out new content about SlideShare on LinkedIn.com

☑ **Share my activity with my connections on LinkedIn.com**
  ☑ Display my SlideShare uploads on LinkedIn.com
  ☑ Display my SlideShare "likes" on LinkedIn news feed

Save Settings

The process is extremely easy. Simply select one of the two available themes (there may be more in the future) and publish! Here is what my Professional Journey looks like (http://www.slideshare.net/theessayexpert/professional-journey-the-essay-expert-llc)

2 SlideShare Professional Journey - https://www.slideshare.net/professional-journey

Here is how it will appear on your connections' homepage feed:

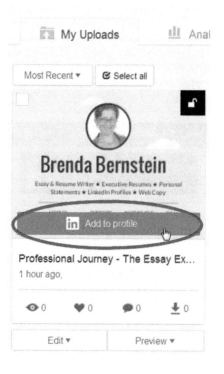

You can then share your presentation with your LinkedIn connections and also publish it to your profile by going to your My Uploads page, hovering over the presentation and clicking Add to profile.

Results to Expect

Your profile will be a multi-media event! Readers will have fun scrolling through your profile and be impressed that you utilized LinkedIn's technology to its full advantage.

By sharing your events, relevant reading, presentations, videos, documents, and resume in your Portfolio, you will remain a current and savvy LinkedIn user who attracts attention to your profile. A well-utilized Portfolio can lead to interest from both employers and customers who click on your links.

Playing the LinkedIn Game to Win

Having a KILLER LinkedIn® Profile is just the beginning. You then need to use it!

You could sit there with a keyword-optimized profile hoping for recruiters to contact you, and someday they might do that . . .

You could fly solo, not joining or participating in groups...

You could laze around and hope your contacts are inspired to recommend you...

You could write your profile and let it idle there for years, thinking you've fulfilled your LinkedIn duty...

You could do all those things, and maybe someone would contact you. But it's unlikely.

Instead, be proactive in using LinkedIn's Jobs functions and reaching out to your networking contacts. Join groups and leverage opportunities to share, learn and connect. Risk asking your connections to endorse and recommend you.

Your LinkedIn profile is a living, breathing creation that requires attention and care. This section shows you how to treat it that way so you experience KILLER results from your LinkedIn presence!

MISTAKE #15

Not Utilizing LinkedIn's Jobs Functions

The Problem

Whether you are a job seeker or an employer, you need to know about LinkedIn Jobs. Jobs are so important on LinkedIn, in fact, that they have their own tab right in the top menu. Mobile apps for iOS and Android mean job seekers can apply to jobs using LinkedIn right from their phones. A partnership with the data-driven matching technology company Bright makes LinkedIn increasingly powerful as a center for connecting talent with opportunity.

LinkedIn is becoming the #1 resource for job listings on the web and if you're not on this bandwagon it's time to jump on!

The Tune-Up

The simplest step to take with LinkedIn Jobs is simply to click on Jobs in the top menu. There are also Job Discussions in your LinkedIn Group that could be fruitful sources of new employment!

Job Seekers

Under the Jobs tab, you will automatically see a list of jobs that might interest you, based on the keywords in your profile.

I recommend that as a job seeker, you click on the Jobs tab daily. But don't stop there. Use the Advanced Search feature to search for the jobs you want in the geographic area that interests you. You can also expand your criteria by country, industry, area and job function using the Advanced search feature. (Note that searching by salary is only available to Premium members.)

Once your criteria are entered, LinkedIn will provide a list of current positions which you can sort by relevance, relationship, most recent and oldest job postings. When I searched for Account Executive Digital Media within 100 miles of Madison, WI, here's some of what came up:

If this is a search you want to conduct regularly, click on Save search in the upper right hand corner and you will be given an option to receive an alert daily, weekly or monthly for jobs that match your search criteria.

Enter your title and preferred alert frequency, then click the green checkmark to save.

Saved Searches

Type	Title	New	Alert	Created
Jobs	Account Executive Digital Media		Weekly	✓ ⊗

You have no saved searches.

Tip: You can currently save up to 10 job searches to easily access from the results page.
LinkedIn can automatically run your search and email you the new results.

Close

You will then receive job postings in your inbox and you will be able to conduct your saved search with one click from your Jobs page:

Saved jobs (0)   ★

Save jobs you're interested in and get back to them later.

Saved searches (1)

• Account Executive Digital Media
  0 new results

See all saved searches ▶

Applied jobs

Review your past job applications here.

See all applied jobs ▶

Once you click on a position that interests you, you will see a job description, a count of the number of people who have applied through LinkedIn, and a button to Apply on company website or Save the job:

Apply on company website   Save

Is this job not quite right for you but it might be perfect for someone else in your network? Use LinkedIn social media sharing buttons to spread the word. You can even reach out to find out more about the job from the person who posted it. Or, take a look at similar jobs with the People also viewed or Similar jobs features:

Contact the job poster

Reach out for more information or to follow up on your application.

Recruiting Manager at Media...

Send InMail

People also viewed

Publisher Development Manager
Greater New York City Area
Posted 13 days ago

Digital Marketing Consultants...
United Kingdom
Posted 13 days ago

Account Executive Expert
Greater Chicago Area
Posted 4 days ago

Advertising Sales Executive
Greater Chicago Area
Posted 11 days ago

Share   **Tweet** 0   **Like** 0

Similar jobs

Digital Media Consultant
Greater Chicago Area
Posted 15 days ago

Online Media Account
Executive
Austin, Texas Area
Posted 26 days ago

Digital Media Analyst
Greater Chicago Area
Posted 21 days ago

Digital Media/Media
Technology Jobs
Greater New York City...
Posted 27 days ago

Account Executive: Digital
Ad Sales
San Francisco Bay Area
Posted 15 days ago

Digital Media Account
Executive, Marketing &...
Greater Chicago Area
Posted 13 days ago

Advertising Sales
Orlando, Florida Area
Posted 14 days ago

Online Advertising Yield
Manager
Greater Chicago Area
Posted 28 days ago

Note: If you want a company to know you are interested in working for them, follow the company on LinkedIn! Hiring entities that use LinkedIn Recruiter can view those who follow their company. They will then consider you a "warm lead" and most likely check out your profile. Plus, you can follow up to 1,000 companies! The downside is that all your connections will also be able to see what companies you follow; so if you have an ummm, "overprotective" boss, be careful about how you use this feature.

Another key location for potential jobs is the Jobs Discussions in your groups. After logging into a group page, click on the Job tab and you will see Job Discussions in the left-hand navigation bar. Click on Job Discussions to see additional positions not advertised in the official (paid) Jobs database.

If you are serious about finding a new job fast, research and apply for jobs on LinkedIn daily. And if you find you want more functionality than you can get with a free account, you might want to consider Job Seeker Premium to get more information on salary range, who is viewing your profile, and what your competition looks like.

For Mobile Job Seekers:

LinkedIn offers the some of the same job search functionality to mobile users as well, so you can keep up with your job search on the go. Don't let that job offer sit in your inbox for hours while you're out networking!

For Android and iOS users:

Download LinkedIn for your mobile device.[1]

To use the LinkedIn application on your iOS or Android:

- Using the LinkedIn app, log into your LinkedIn account.
- Tap the icon in the upper left corner.

---

1 LinkedIn Mobile App - https://www.linkedin.com/mobile

- From the dropdown menu, select Jobs.
- You can then view the jobs that LinkedIn has recommended for your or search for jobs, save your searches, and apply.
- You can also sync your phone with your LinkedIn account.

For iPhone users:

Download the LinkedIn Job Search App for iPhone (iTunes).[2]

iPhone users enjoy additional amenities with the Job Search App for iPhone. Search jobs, save searches, set up notifications, apply online and track jobs you've applied to.

For more about LinkedIn for mobile users, go to: https://www.linkedin.com/mobile.

Employers/Recruiters

If you have a company page on LinkedIn, after clicking on the Jobs tab, you will see an "Are you hiring?" section in the top right corner:

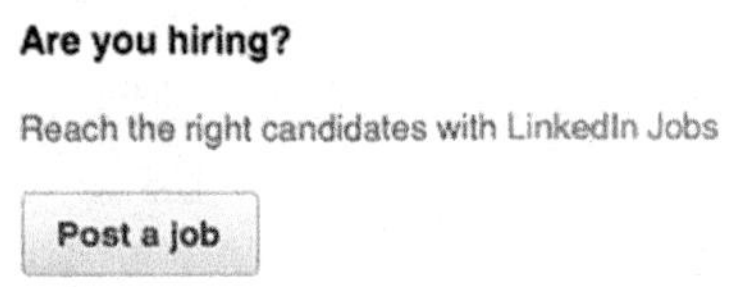

Are you hiring?

Reach the right candidates with LinkedIn Jobs

Post a job

---

2 LinkedIn Job Search App for iPhone (iTunes) - http://tinyurl.com/qcspc38

Click on the Post a job button and you will be brought to another screen where you will also click on Post a Job.

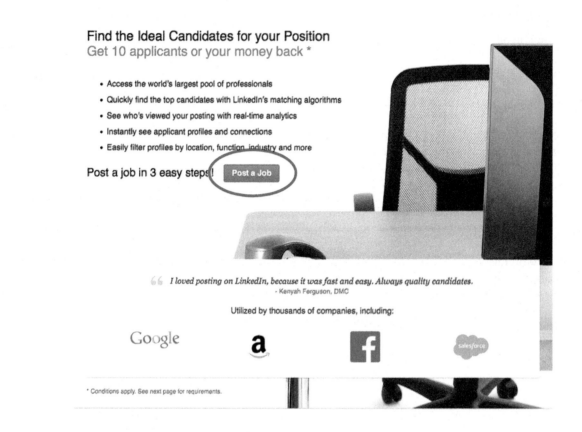

Then you will get a message advising you of the price of a 30-day ad for your geographic area. As an example, in Madison, it costs $199 to post a job for 30 days (less than most local newspaper want ads):

You can also get to this page through the Business Services tab (dropdown item Post a Job).

Posting a job on LinkedIn provides credibility to your company that will attract top candidates. Simply put, in my opinion LinkedIn is the best job board currently in existence. Where else do you get such complete information on both candidates and companies? If I were looking for an employee, I would post the opening on LinkedIn before trying any other advertising venues. Even if referrals are your best source of job candidates, LinkedIn is a central place to get the word out.

The advantages of posting jobs on LinkedIn:

1. You can forward the job posting easily to your 1st degree connections to spread the word and generate referrals.

2. You can share the posting easily with your LinkedIn groups, LinkedIn Network, Facebook and Twitter.

3. You can link a job posting to your profile so that everyone who views your profile sees the job posting.

4. The Profile Match feature provides up to 24 of the best candidates matched to your position.

5. There's a 10-applicant guarantee for members who have not previously posted a job on LinkedIn.

6. When you post a job, an update will go to all your 1st degree connections.

7. Candidates are automatically asked to upload their resume and cover letter. Once someone applies, you get an email with a summary of the applicant's LinkedIn profile and all the documents they submitted; you can then review their full profile if you'd like.

8. When a new applicant applies, you get a link to view all the candidates who have applied for the job to date. You will find this feature very useful!

9. LinkedIn is probably the best database of professionals worldwide in just about any industry. If your candidate is not leveraging LinkedIn, they might not be the right candidate.

> **Note:** If you have purchased a Gold or Silver Career page for your Company page, featured jobs will be displayed on that page and will be targeted to viewers based on how relevant their profile is to the job posted. This function provides tremendous screening value to you as an employer or recruiter.

LinkedIn has also made "limited listings" available to its job-seeking members. Not to be confused with Job Slots or Job Posts which are visible to all job seekers, limited listings are job listings aggregated from sources outside of LinkedIn that are displayed only to members who are the most relevant candidates for the position, based on their profile content and the employer's criteria.[3]

---

3 Starting A Test To Add More Job Listings To LinkedIn — Here's What You Should Know - http://tinyurl.com/ojtwshk

Free Job Postings

You can post jobs for free using the Job Discussions feature in your groups. After logging into one of your group pages, click on the Discussions tab and post your job opening. You will have an option to select Job next to the Discussion type option. Click Share and if the group is moderated, the owner will be notified. If accepted, the job will appear in the Job Discussions section of your group.

Results to Expect

The evidence, based on my own client base, is that more and more qualified job seekers are finding employment by diligently applying for jobs on LinkedIn. This is good news for both applicants and employers. Whether you are looking for a position or looking to fill one, LinkedIn is a powerful tool to achieve your intended result.

If you are a job seeker, and if you look in LinkedIn Jobs daily and apply for positions appropriate to your background, you will likely see results! I have one client who got 12 interviews that way, and a job!

MISTAKE #16

Insufficient or Ineffective Group Membership

LinkedIn groups are communities of individuals with similar interests or a particular professional common ground. There are groups for people who are job seekers (which also contain recruiters and employers); groups for people with particular technical knowledge; and groups for lawyers, project managers, graduates from various schools, and even cooks.

Once you join a group, you have access to Discussions and Job Postings relevant to that group, and you yourself can post discussions and answer questions asked in the group.

According to a July 2014 report by Zephoria, there are over 2.1 million groups on LinkedIn and on average, each user is a member of 7 groups. You can choose to join up to 50 LinkedIn groups.

The Problem

LinkedIn groups can provide you with access to thousands of potential readers. If you're not a member of groups relevant to you, you won't be reaching the people you want to reach, and your networking opportunities will be severely limited. You will not get the value that's available from LinkedIn.

As business consultant Laurie Phillips states, "Group memberships and activity gives me a clue about whether the candidate is building a broad business network, as well as what topics/organizations they associate with closely. It's a great source for insight on someone before I meet with them."

If you're not a member of a robust number of groups you will miss out on the opportunity to provide valuable information to the people who view your profile.

The Tune-Up

Search for and join groups where you will connect with your target audience. For instance, if you are seeking a job in the IT industry, join IT-related groups and job-seeking groups such as Linked:HR that contain recruiters. If you provide services to small businesses, join groups such as the Small Business Forum. If you provide services to children, join groups that contain parents.

You will then have access to the people you want to reach. There are several ways to find groups to join:

1. CONDUCT AN ADVANCED SEARCH IN GROUPS.

To do this, first click on the drop down menu to the left of the search bar and select Groups:

Then, in the search box, type the search terms that are relevant to you, and a list of groups will come up sorted by groups with the most members first. I typed "Project Manager" into the group search bar and here's just some of what I found:

2. JOIN GROUPS BASED ON WHO IS IN THEM.

Are there people you particularly respect on LinkedIn? Perhaps they are members of groups you would want to belong to. When you view someone's profile, you can view their group membership unless they have hidden this information. For example:

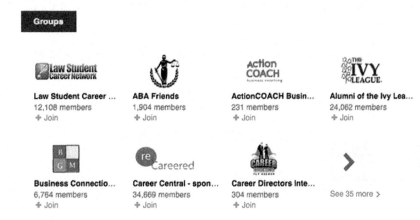

3. USE THE CONVERSATION FEED.

LinkedIn provides a feed consisting of discussions posted to every group you are a member of, and even suggests conversations from non member groups based on your current group choices.

There's no need to navigate to a group page in order to post. Simply create your content and select which group you would like to share it with. Note that you can only share with one group at a time, which is LinkedIn's way of reducing spam.

As you can see, LinkedIn makes it easy to join groups directly from anyone's profile.

GENERAL ADVICE ON JOINING GROUPS:

Before joining a group, check the number of members. Ideally you will join a mix of groups, some with membership in the thousands and some smaller ones. Groups with only a few hundred members might get you more attention if you post something, since there are not as many people posting. I have personally found the members of local groups tend to respond more often to my posts than people in bigger groups with wider membership.

There are hundreds of thousands of members in many groups! If you're looking to greatly expand your network, you might want to join one of these mammoth connector groups (LION is one of them) and start making invitations.

To join a group, just click Join. You will either be automatically accepted into the group, or your request will go to a moderator who will approve or deny your request. Most of the time you will be approved.

Once you join a group, don't just sit there . . . do something! Here's the menu you'll find under each group:

Go to Discussions and share articles relevant to your groups (you can share any article from the web, along with a comment or question, by using the Sharing Bookmarklet described in Mistake #12, or by sharing any update of interest by clicking Share). Start discussions that the group will find interesting. Respond to other people's comments in discussions. Post news articles. Put yourself out there. Then let the group take your conversations and run with them.

Also, connect with people if you like their comments in a discussion. You can make long-lasting connections this way and maybe even get some help with an issue you're facing. I recommend setting up a phone call or coffee date to really get to know the people in your group who could be valuable connections.

> **HINT:** When you share group membership with someone, you can send them a message without being connected. To message a group member, click on the Members tab within the group, then search for the person's name. An option to "Send Message" will appear below each group member's profile. You can join a group for the sole purpose of communicating with someone with whom communication would otherwise be difficult. Once you connect with the person, you can leave the group! Note that you can only send 15 messages per month of this type, so choose wisely.

> **BIG HINT:** If you're looking to stand out and be noticed on LinkedIn, prioritize participating in discussions where there are already a LOT of comments — over 100 at least. Most of those people will be following the discussion and will therefore get an email when a new comment is posted. That means they will read your comment — and if you impress them they might soon be asking you for help!

Participation gets you noticed. If your goal is effective networking, your participation, more than how many groups you've joined, is what's important. Active participation in a small number of groups is far better for your networking health than lack of participation in a large number of groups.

> **Note:** If you are a member of a group but don't want the public to know for any reason, you can hide the groups in your list. Go to "Your Groups," click on the icon for the group you want to hide, and you will get the following menu:

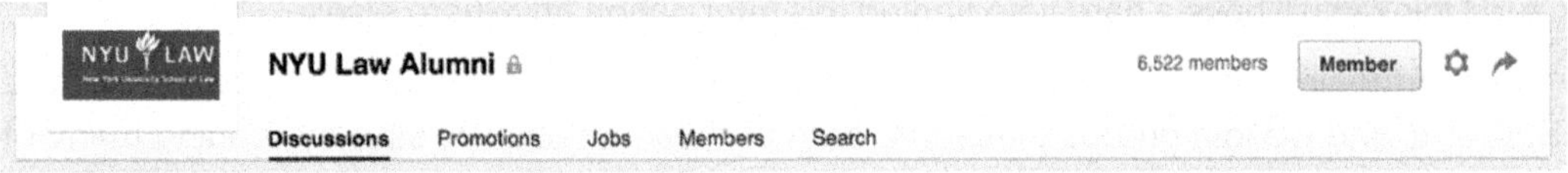

Click on the gear icon and you will see the following screen:

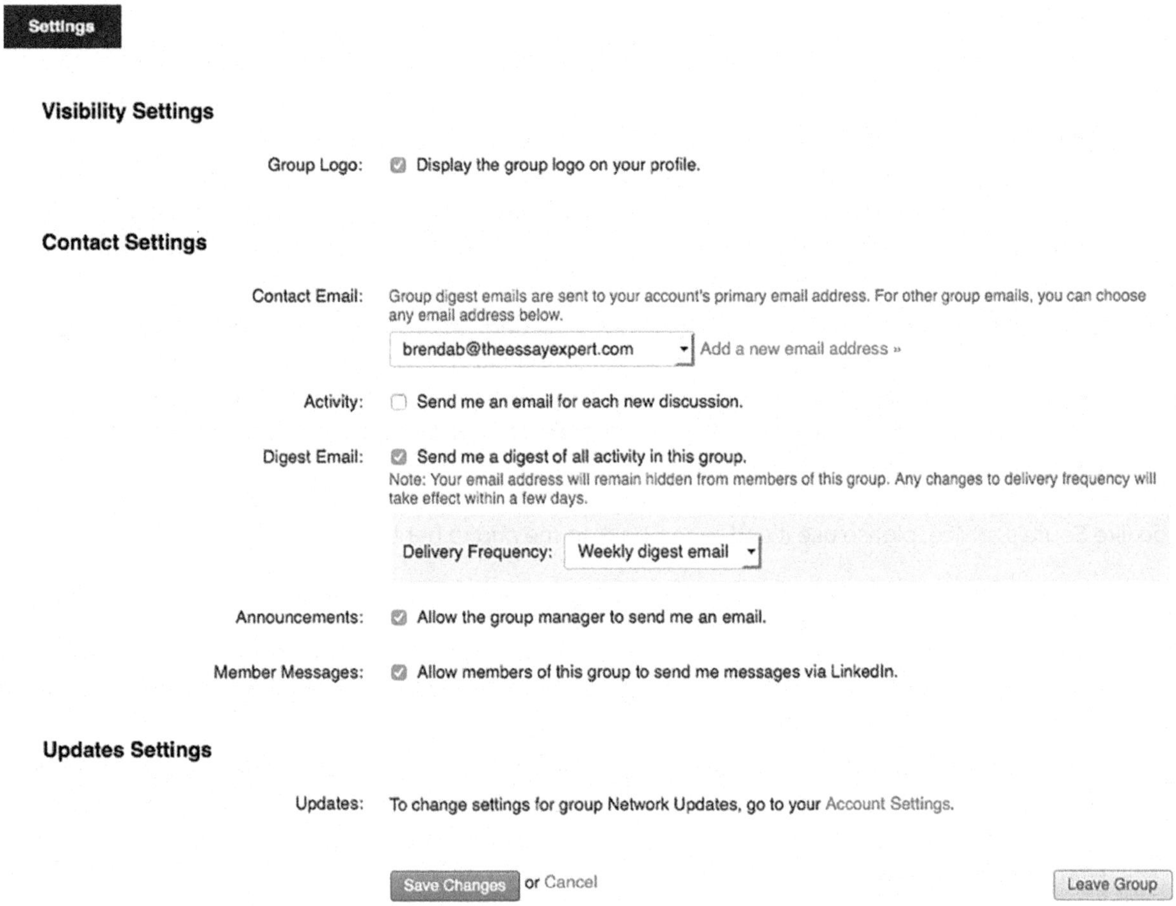

To hide a group, uncheck the box next to Group Logo: "Display the group logo on my profile."

You can manage the frequency of emails that you receive from a group from this screen. I recommend weekly instead of daily digests, since the email traffic can be heavy! You can also choose not to receive updates from certain groups if you are feeling overwhelmed by the volume of email you are receiving.

SPECIAL TIP FOR MARKETERS!

In one of my group discussions, Saura Johnston of Your Business Allies[1] shared the following great insights and tips for companies wanting to market to group members. She gave me permission to reprint her post in my book and I think you'll have a hard time finding this information anywhere else:

> "Most of the value I gain from LinkedIn is from Groups. Our company has both a B2B and B2C arm, and we join groups that serve both of these needs. We start by reading many of the discussions and selecting the most valuable contributors. We comment and contribute to many discussions, and bring value to the discussions overall. Then, we visit the profiles of the best contributors, and see what other groups they are part of. This always leads to similar groups that serve our needs. We join these groups, identify key contributors, add value, and see their groups as well.

> Then we start delivering valued content to the best groups. We try to match the tone, concerns and interests of the groups. It helps to start by listening first, and by joining in discussions first, because you can really get a feel for the culture of the group.

> As we build relationships in the groups, we will ask to connect with key members—best contributors, potential customers, and leaders. It is important to note that the top contributors and those that most frequently comment are not necessarily the valuable players in the group. It is important to read what people are saying and weigh it against your goals for the group.

> Group marketing strategy takes consistency and dedication. When you post, you need to respond quickly to comments and questions. You need to post often enough to build a reputation, but not so often that you are spam. You need to always deliver valuable content and add value to the discussions on other people's content. Groups are already targeted for you by interest, so we love them!"

If you like Saura's advice, please use it and report back to me and to her how it went!

Results to Expect

1. According to Link Humans, "your profile is 5 times more likely to be viewed if you join and are active in groups." Joining groups and participating in discussions are your keys to accessing the power of LinkedIn. Here are some reasons why:

2. The more comments a discussion generates, the higher up it will appear in the daily and weekly digests sent out by the group—and the more people will start to pay attention. If you start a discussion that generates 100 or more comments, you will gain credibility and interest; people will want to connect with you and know who you are.

3. If your discussion is posted at the right time (which varies from group to group), your discussion might end up at the top of the daily or weekly digest.

---

1 Your Business Allies - https://www.linkedin.com/company/your-business-allies

4. People will come to you to do business. I know this really happens because it happened to me. When a discussion I started about grammar generated over 225 comments, I had people writing to me and saying, "I love the discussion you posted. My company could really use your services." Or, "I learned so much from your article. Can you help me with my resume?" Or even simply, "I showed your article to my son and my husband. They both learned a ton!" Not only did my discussion generate business for my company, but it also gave me the satisfaction of knowing I was making a difference for people's writing. And the mother who wrote to me might think of me when her son is ready to apply to college.

5. You will make connections with potential business partners. This also happened to me. When I wrote an email to someone who had written a great comment on my blog, we struck up a conversation about teaching business writing classes together. And when someone else contacted me wanting writing coaching for his employees, I had something to offer him.

6. If you have a web page, web site or blog, watch the increase in traffic as you begin to establish yourself in your LinkedIn groups. That's what every web site owner wants!

No Recommendations, Very Few Recommendations, and/or Boring or Error-Filled Recommendations

You have the opportunity on LinkedIn to request recommendations from people you know: your colleagues, clients, supervisors, or even staff. You will find the option to request or offer recommendations after you click on Profile; just scroll down to your Recommendations section.

Recommendations   Ask to be recommended   Manage

With the advent of Endorsements (for more about Endorsements, see Mistake #11), it might be tempting to rely on those easily checked boxes and become complacent about requesting more personal recommendations. Don't be lulled! Endorsements take no energy on the part of the person making the endorsement, and sometimes people who cannot actually vouch for your skills endorse you for those skills.

The Problem

Many LinkedIn members have plentiful recommendations in addition to their Endorsements; if you do not, people might wonder whether they can truly trust you. In the past, at least one recommendation was required to have a 100% complete profile! There is also some evidence that search results are ranked partly by how many recommendations you have. Fewer recommendations can mean lower ranking.

As Laurie Phillips, business consultant and CEO at Sundance Research, offers: "Even if candidates don't give me their LinkedIn profile link, I check them out here [because] LinkedIn gives me descriptive personal references that corporations typically prohibit. Even though I know those references are biased toward the positive, they give me some idea of your personality."

Errors and poor writing, or simply a lack of spark in your recommendations, reflect poorly on both you and the recommender – and the recommendation can backfire.

The Tune-Up

Don't be shy. Write to the people you have worked with and ask them to recommend you on LinkedIn. If you own a business or are looking for work, it is especially important to use this opportunity to have people sell you – so you don't have to do all the selling yourself.

I recommend displaying at least 3 recommendations, with 5-10 being ideal for most professionals. There are three ways to initiate a recommendation request:

OPTION #1:

From your Profile, scroll down to the Recommendations section and click on the Ask to be Recommended button:

Recommendations   Ask to be recommended   Manage

OPTION #2:

Click on the Manage button:

Recommendations   Ask to be recommended   Manage

Then on the following page, click on the Ask for recommendations tab.

Recommendations

Received (7)   Given   **Ask for recommendations (60)**   Give recommendations (14)

OPTION #3:

Go to Privacy & Settings. On the Profile tab, click on Manage your recommendations under Helpful Links.

Profile	Privacy Controls	Settings
Communications	Turn on/off your activity broadcasts	Manage your Twitter settings
	Select who can see your activity feed	Manage your WeChat settings
Groups, Companies & Applications	Select what others see when you've viewed their profile	**Helpful Links**
	Turn on/off How You Rank	Edit your name, location & industry »
Account	Select who can see your connections	Edit your profile »
	Choose who can follow your updates	Edit your public profile »
	Change your profile photo & visibility »	Manage your recommendations »
	Show/hide "Viewers of this profile also viewed" box	
	Manage who you're blocking »	
	Manage who can discover you by your phone number »	

Click on the Ask for recommendations tab. You will be brought to the following screen:

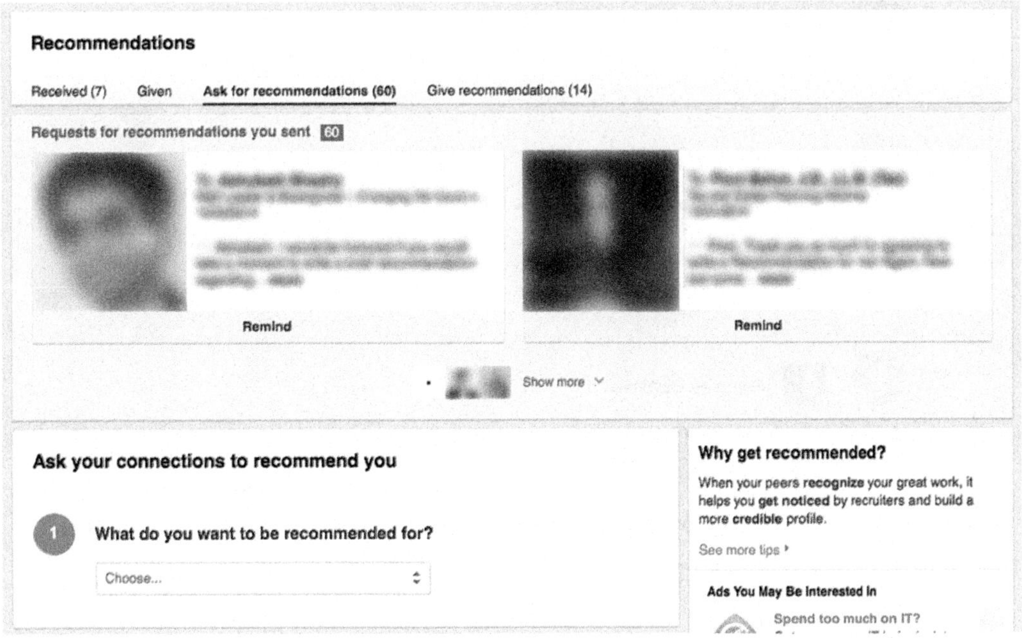

You will be required to provide the following information:

1. Which position you would like to be recommended for

2. From whom you'd like to ask the recommendation

3. What your relationship with that connection is

4. What your connection's position was at the time

Only after providing these details will you be ready to create a message requesting the recommendation.

Ask your connections to recommend you

(1) **What do you want to be recommended for?**

> Executive Resume Writer, LinkedIn Trainer, Colleg ⇕

(2) **Who do you want to ask?**

Your connections: (You can add up to 3 people)

> Jeanne ⊕ Goodman ✕

(3) ▨ Jeanne ⊕ Goodman

What's your relationship?

> You were a client of Jeanne　　　⇕

What was Jeanne's position at the time?

> ✦ Virtual Assistant and Website Technician at Life ⇕

(4) **Write your message**

Subject:

> Can you recommend me?

> I'm writing to ask if you would write a brief recommendation of my work that I can include on my LinkedIn profile. If you have any questions, please let me know.
>
> Thanks in advance for your help.
>
> -Brenda Bernstein

[Send]　[Cancel]

Don't simply use the default message there ("I'm writing to ask if you would write a brief recommendation of my work that I can include on my LinkedIn profile. If you have any questions, please let me know. Thanks in advance for your help.")

Instead, say hello to the person and ask how he or she is doing (or, ideally, do this by phone before asking for the recommendation at all). If you haven't been in contact for some time, remind this colleague, boss, or other connection of a project you worked on together, a deal you made, or something else that will refresh their recollection of your professional skills. Then ask your recommender to tell a clear, specific story or two about you (positive ones of course). Examples of how you handled a situation, what you accomplished, or how you helped someone are always more informative and interesting than generalizations!

Consider, if you have more than 10 recommendations, whether you are displaying too many (the answer to this question will depend on your situation). If I applied at your company and gave you 150 letters of recommendation, how much attention would you pay to each one?

You can save all recommendations and display the ones you choose at any given time. You may choose to display certain recommendations when job seeking, others when starting a new business.

To show or hide your recommendations, go to the Received tab and you will be able to manage your recommendations:

The default is to "show" the recommendation. If you do not want to display it, uncheck the "show" box by clicking it and the recommendation will be hidden (see above example).

I encourage you to recommend people as well as to request recommendations. It feels great to help someone out, and all your connections will get notified that you recommended someone. However, make sure to have some "one-way" recommendations, as "mutual" or "reciprocal" recommendations are often not as highly trusted.

Want to request a "replacement" recommendation? Hover over the pending recommendation and an option to Ask for changes will appear:

If there is an error or something you'd rather that someone say differently, ask your recommender to correct it. Make sure each recommendation says something compelling about you – that it tells a story of some sort and could not have been written about anyone else. Most people are very cooperative when you make a request for a replacement – remember, the recommendations say as much about the recommender as they do about you! If you're afraid to request a replacement, just tell them I sent you.

Here's a before and after example from one of my clients:

Before: "Besides really enjoying the time with Mary, her knowledge of Networking opportunities were invaluable. We related very well and her training techniques were easy to follow. This opened up a whole new world of networking opportunity which will be pursue with vigor. I look forward to continuing a working relationship with her."

After: "Not only was Mary enjoyable to work with, but her knowledge of Networking was invaluable. We related very well and her training techniques were easy to follow. She opened up a whole new world of networking opportunities which our company will pursue with vigor."

Of course this tip applies to you as well if you are writing a recommendation. Craft it well, as it reflects on you as much as on the person you're recommending. Only recommend people whose work you truly know!

Here are some issues that commonly come up with people on my LinkedIn webinars:

1. **"I haven't talked to my recommender in 10 years . . . I would be so embarrassed to ask!"**

   In this situation, think about how you would respond if the tables were turned. Wouldn't you be happy to hear from someone who did good work for you or who was a great boss or colleague 10 years ago? If you thought highly of the person, wouldn't you be happy to provide a recommendation? And seriously, what's the worst that can happen? They don't respond or they say no? In that case, you won't be any worse off than you are without their recommendation now!

2. **"My recommenders aren't on LinkedIn."**

   In this situation, there are at least three options that can address the issue:

   • Invite the person onto LinkedIn. It might be just the nudge your recommender needs to join the millions of LinkedIn users!

   • Attach your recommendation under the relevant job as a link or file, using the instructions in Mistake #14. If you do this, you may want to write a line in that section directing readers to view your attached recommendations.

- Include the recommendation in the summary or experience section of your profile. Most people will trust that it's real, though some might be more trusting of a recommendation that comes through LinkedIn's official Recommendations system. If the comment is persuasive and flows in the context of the section, I say go ahead and type it in! Here's an example of what it might look like (at the end of the Summary) from Robin Rice of Be Who You Are Productions, Inc.:

AUTHOR • TOP LEVEL PERSONAL CONSULTANT • THOUGHT LEADER • PROBLEM SOLVER

Robin's seven books have been published in three languages and distributed in nine countries and have introduced audiences around the world to groundbreaking ideas. Called a "rainmaker" by many of her clients, her seminars, apprenticeships and travel abroad programs regularly sell out, and her annual social change projects and media have transformed lives around the world.

"Robin does not think outside the box. She thinks in the exact center of the box."

"From my personal experience with Robin, I see her strongest gift as showing you your way, not hers. This is enormously liberating."

> **NOTE:** There are three downsides to these last two options: Theoretically you could make the recommendation up; it is harder for viewers to find the recommendation; and the recommendation will not be counted by LinkedIn so will not show up in your number of recommendations received.

3. **"My previous company has a policy against recommendations."**

If your past supervisors are precluded from recommending you due to company policy, you might have hit a dead end—but your coworkers might still be able to write a recommendation; and keep track of those supervisors, as they might move to a new company and be freed up to write a recommendation for you. Pay attention to the daily emails you receive with updates and look for news about potential recommenders!

Note that some supervisors, even if they are not officially permitted to recommend you, might sign a letter of recommendation that you draft for them. Or if you present such a letter to them, they might decide to write one themselves. This type of thing happens more often than you think! So even if you can't extract a public LinkedIn recommendation from someone, see if you can get an old-fashioned letter!

Results to Expect

Your Recommendations section will look something like this:

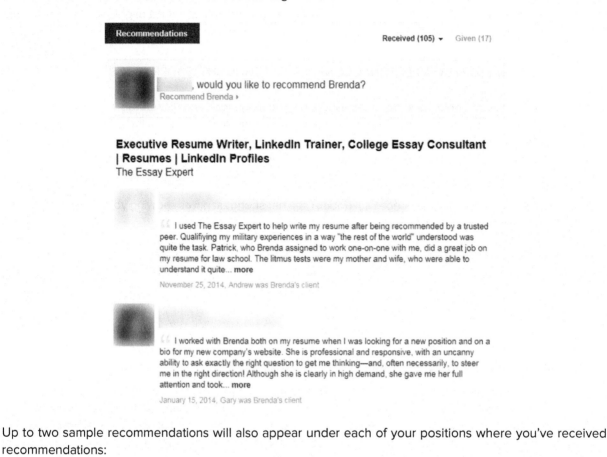

Up to two sample recommendations will also appear under each of your positions where you've received recommendations:

If you prefer to display recommendations other than the ones that appear by default, you can hide them; but then no one will be able to view the hidden recommendations and they will NOT be counted in the number of recommendations displayed on your profile.

By accumulating recommendations, you will gain the trust of potential employers, clients, and whomever else you want to impress on LinkedIn—trust that can translate into business or into a job. I have had many people choose to work with The Essay Expert based on the strength of the recommendations posted on my LinkedIn profile. Imagine, if you are a business or sales person, having clients come to you already having decided you're the person they want to work with!

If your recommendations are compelling and error-free, both you and your recommenders will make a great impression. The strength of your recommendations can get you your next client or your next job.

A Static (Unchanging, Outdated) Profile – and thinking all you need is a KILLER LinkedIn profile

The Problem

Your LinkedIn profile is not a static, unchanging document. Members expect to find up to date information there! You wouldn't send out a resume without your most current position listed, or with past positions listed as if they are current. Why would you have a LinkedIn profile with outdated information?

If you earned a degree in 2014 and haven't worked since 2011, it would be a shame to forget to list those three years you were in school! You could appear to be unemployed when you really were a hard-working student that whole time.

Every time you update your profile, a message goes out to all your connections (unless your Activity Broadcasts are turned off). If you don't update your profile, you are missing out on an opportunity to be noticed.

Likewise, even if you have the most amazing LinkedIn profile in the world, you won't get results by sitting there doing nothing.

The Tune-Up

Make sure your Headline, Summary, Experience (Job Titles) and Education sections are regularly updated. Update your accomplishments when you achieve new ones. Join new groups. Make and request new recommendations. Post links and Activity Updates relevant to who you are and what you're up to. Stay active.

If you are afraid you are making *too* many changes, and that your connections will get annoyed, make sure your notifications are turned off when you save your profile changes. You can access this feature from the right sidebar of your profile editing page:

Notify your network?

No, do not publish an update to my network about my profile changes.　　No

Or, go to the Account & Settings tab, which you will find under your photo name in the right hand corner of your homepage:

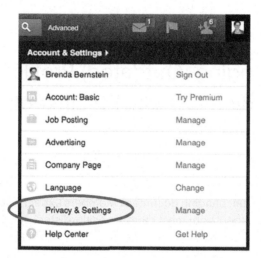

Click on Privacy & Settings and you have access to all your privacy settings.

If you tend to forget that your LinkedIn profile exists, you might want to put a tickler in your calendar reminding you to update your profile at least every month. Also, read articles about new features on LinkedIn and about how to write a great profile. Update your profile according to what you learn. Reading this book – and keeping up with future editions – is a great first step!

LinkedIn has Android and iPhone apps so you can even update your profile from your cell phone! Check out LinkedIn Blog's Profile Edit on the Go![1]

Finally, unless you stay active in groups, discussions, and . . . most important . . . OFF LINE, you will not get the greatest possible results out of your LinkedIn Profile!

---

1 Profile Edit on the Go! - http://blog.linkedin.com/2012/11/13/profile-edit-on-the-go-video/

LinkedIn provides a wealth of information about every one of your contacts. Be an explorer!

Read through someone's entire profile before starting a conversation. You may discover videos and other documents in addition to basic education and employment information. If they completed an Interests section, you'll get a sense of who they are out of the office. If they have recommended people you can get insight into their values system. If they have received multiple recommendations you'll get a sense of their greatest strengths. Do they volunteer somewhere? If so, talking about their volunteer experience can be a great icebreaker.

Look on the right-hand side of anyone's profile to see how you're connected and what you have in common. Then use that information to make a connection!

Pay attention to your Connections page (dropdown item Keep in Touch) where you get notifications of people's birthdays and job changes/anniversaries. Respond to them!

Don't forget to write comments, post questions, give and receive recommendations and endorsements . . . and ask people you want to truly connect with to talk with you on the phone or even meet you for coffee or lunch!

Results to Expect

By staying updated and active, you will likely get emails congratulating you on your new position, your new accomplishment, or the new look of your profile. You will be seen as someone who is active in your profession and serious about your online presentation. Not only that, but if you comment on people's news, they will **like** you! Who doesn't appreciate getting congratulated or being wished a happy birthday?

The more activity you generate, the more people will view your profile and the more likely you are to make connections.

I'll tell you a secret: A huge proportion of my business was built because I was active in a group and the manager of the group connected me with one of its other members who lives in Austin, Texas. I happened to be visiting Austin and met with that member, and he was so impressed with our meeting that he began referring me multiple clients and giving me opportunities to present webinars with his company.

Please take that story to heart. Don't stop at online LinkedIn connections! Bring them to the next level with a phone call or in-person meeting, and the possibilities are endless.

See how you're doing at making business connections by checking your Social Selling Index[2]. According to LinkedIn, "salespeople who excel at social selling are creating more opportunities and are 51% more likely to hit quota."[3]

---

2 LinkedIn's Social Selling Index - http://tinyurl.com/phkq9vh

3 How Sales Reps Exceed Quota, Make Club and Get Promoted Faster - http://tinyurl.com/p8ykekh

Here's what your score will look like:

To find out more about this feature, read How Sales Reps Exceed Quota, Make Club and Get Promoted Faster[4] from the LinkedIn® Sales Solutions Blog.

BONUS TIP #1

Save Your Work . . . and Your Connections!

The Problem

LinkedIn is not a perfect system, and there have been stories of disappearing profiles. If you haven't saved the results of all your hard work, you can lose it. I'm guessing that would be aggravating for you. Furthermore, if your profile gets axed for any reason, you could easily lose your hundreds or thousands of LinkedIn connections.

The Tune-Up

To retain the results of your labors, back up your profile!

LinkedIn has created a way for you to save all of your information in one fell swoop by requesting an archive of your data.

To request your archive, go to your Privacy & Settings and click the Account tab:

Click the Request archive button on the right:

Request your data archive

Download your LinkedIn data
You can request an archive of all your activity and data on LinkedIn anytime. It'll take about 72 hours for us to compile it. Once we do, you'll get an email with a link where you can download it. You'll also be able to access your archive by going to your settings, selecting the Account tab, and clicking **Request an archive of your data**. To learn more, visit our Help Center.

What's included?
Your data archive will include all the information LinkedIn has stored about you that you can't access in other ways, including all your activity and account history, from who invited you to join, to the time of your latest login. For the full list, visit our Help Center.

You will then see the following screen:

Success! You'll get an email within 72 hours with a link to download your archive.

What's on its way? You'll get all the information LinkedIn has stored about you that you can't access in other ways, including all your activity and account history, from who invited you to join to the last time you logged in. For the full list, visit our Help Center.

Request pending

LinkedIn will also send you a message letting you know that an archive has been requested:

> **Linked in**™
>
> **Hi Brenda,**
>
> We recently got a request for an archive of your data on LinkedIn. It's ready! You can download it with this link. The archive will expire after 72 hours. Because the archive may contain personal information, be sure to keep the link private and only download the archive to your own computer.
>
> Thanks,
> The LinkedIn Team
>
> If you need assistance or have questions, please contact LinkedIn Customer Service. This email was intended for Brenda Bernstein (Essay & Resume Writer ★ Executive Resumes ★ Personal Statements ★ LinkedIn Profiles ★ Web Copy). Learn why we included this. If you need assistance or have questions, please contact LinkedIn Customer Service.
>
> ? 2015, LinkedIn Corporation. 2029 Stierlin Ct. Mountain View, CA 94043, USA

I received my download file within 24 hours and was excited to see all of the information it contained! Here is a list (taken from LinkedIn's help center article regarding downloading your account data)[1]:

Account information:
- Registration information
- Login history including IP records
- Email address history and statuses
- Account history including account closures and reopens

Other information:
- Name information including the current name on your account and any previous name changes
- A list of your 1st degree connections
- Photos that have been uploaded to your account
- Endorsements you've received
- List of skills on your profile

---

1 Accessing Your Account Data - http://tinyurl.com/pdeprt4

- Recommendations given and received
- Group contributions
- Your search history
- Content you've posted, shared, liked, or commented on
- Mobile apps you've installed
- Ads you've clicked on
- The targeting criteria LinkedIn uses to show you ads

I personally discovered:

1. My LinkedIn account was created 5/21/08 and I was invited by an old acquaintance, to whom I wrote a quick thank you as soon as I got my archive!
2. This is a great way to export a connections list (see Exporting Connections Only below)!
3. At the time I requested this archive, I had created 1940 group posts!

Exporting Profile Only

On your View Profile page (in the Profile dropdown), click on the arrow next to Edit and there will be a dropdown with an option Save to PDF.

Save the document that gets generated and you will instantly have a record of all the fruits of your labors. Repeat this export process every time you make a change to your profile.

> **Note:** If you took my advice about inserting graphics into your profile, you might be surprised to see a bunch of hash (#) signs where your beautiful graphics used to be. That's the price of beauty I suppose! Don't be frightened; this is just a little LinkedIn quirk.

Exporting Connections Only

To save your LinkedIn connections, click on Connections and look in the upper right-hand corner for the gear icon:

In the upper right of the following page, find Export LinkedIn Connections.

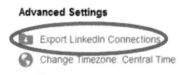

Click on the link to reach a page with the option to export your list to a .csv file.

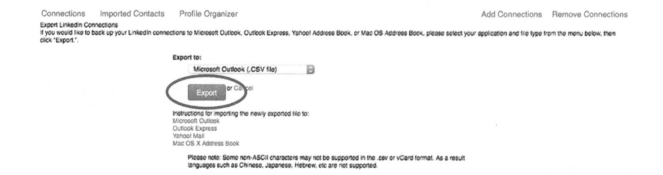

Click on Export, enter the security verification code, and choose Save File. You should then be able to open the file in Excel or whichever spreadsheet program you use.

You will then have the first name, last name and email address of every person in your LinkedIn contact list. Do NOT use this list to send out spam emails! Be courteous please.

> **Note:** If you are exporting your connections to a Mac and you use Mac mail, connections will export directly to your address book (not an Excel spreadsheet). When prompted to import them into your contacts, you may think you are duplicating them, however, they will be saved as a "Smart Group." For more instructions on exporting connections to your Mac, read **How to Manually Import LinkedIn Contacts into Mac Contacts.**[2]

Results to Expect

A recoverable profile and a secure contacts list. Peace of mind.

BONUS TIP #2

For Businesses: Ensure Brand Consistency— and Create a Company Page

The Problem

If you own a company, you want your employees to have profiles that build your brand. If they are misspelling your company name or creating job descriptions willy-nilly, you lose out on brand consistency.

And if all you have on LinkedIn is a personal profile and the personal profiles of your employees, how will people find your company? They certainly won't find you when searching the company pages.

More than 4 million companies have LinkedIn Company Pages. If you're not one of them, you are missing out not just on LinkedIn searchability but on Google search results, where your rankings will suffer.

The Tune-Up

Take some time to create consistency across your employees' profiles. I don't advocate becoming "Big Brother" and keeping close watch at all times over the people working at your company; LinkedIn is indeed a job search tool and I believe you have to accept that employees might use it for that purpose. (My philosophy: Focus on keeping your employees happy rather than preventing them from exploring other opportunities!) More important in my book is that you create a culture of trust by working together with your teams to create a consistent brand and to form community on LinkedIn. Build optimized profiles for company leadership, for all existing employees, and for all new employees, and continue to train your staff on LinkedIn best practices. I believe the benefits to your company will outweigh any risks. A great article on this topic from Forbes is Why Every Employee At Your Company Should Use LinkedIn.[1]

In addition to building consistent management and staff profiles, you must have a company page. To do this, go to the Interests menu and choose Companies from the drop down menu.

---

1 Why Every Employee at Your Company Should Use LinkedIn - http://tinyurl.com/olfltpd

You will be brought to a screen that looks like this:

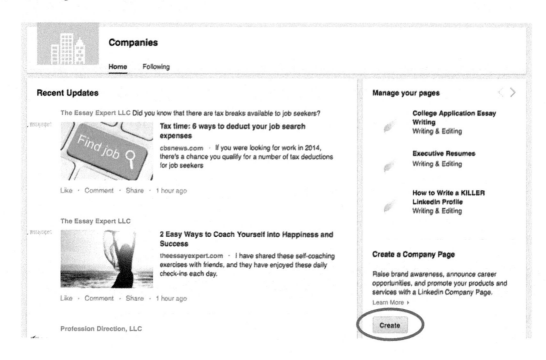

Click the Create button on the right, and you can create your company profile. Note: You must have a company email address (@yourcompany.com) in order to create a company profile. You will not be permitted to use an address with a domain like Yahoo or Gmail.

LinkedIn users can now follow companies' status updates. This feature gives you an opportunity to post a status update for your company just as you would for yourself and to keep your followers informed of all your latest news! You can even target different audiences and track metrics on your posts. Some things you might want to share include news/press about your company, job openings or new products/services offered. Keep your posts short and include videos whenever possible.

Use the time or resources you have dedicated to LinkedIn activities to engage in conversation with followers—an essential part of a customer service strategy. Note that you will have to post individual updates by hand, as LinkedIn no longer supports RSS feeds to Company pages.

LinkedIn has made it possible to create a very attractive company profile whether or not you purchase their premium service. But here's what's possible with the premium:

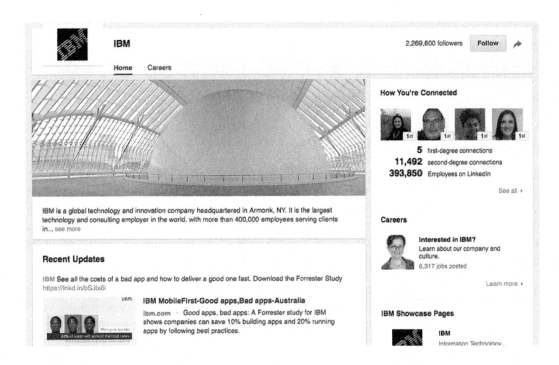

You can promote specialized products or services with Showcase Pages. For example:

Your company can post videos and important updates regarding your featured product/service. You can even identify a specific audience to whom you want to promote it based on company size, job function, industry, seniority, and geography. You can create specific videos tailored to that audience. Interested viewers can follow your page and receive updates in their homepage feed. If you succeed in creating buzz around your offerings you will be well on your way to being a LinkedIn company superstar!

Click the blue arrow below the Edit button to open your Company Admin Center and get great tips on best practices to get the most out of your company page.

According to B2C's article, 10 Things B2B Marketers Should Be Doing On LinkedIn,[2] "over one- third of all impressions were due almost entirely to amplification; that is, people sharing the content you post on your company page out to their network." Taking advantage of this trend, LinkedIn® began rolling out a new product called LinkedIn® Elevate in April 2015. Since the average company employee has 10 times as many connections as their LinkedIn company page has followers, it makes sense for companies to utilize the sharing power of their employers to influence those in their networks as potential customers and hires.

According to LinkedIn's Official Blog article on this topic, "Only 2% of employees share content their company has shared on LinkedIn," yet "they're responsible for about 20% of the overall engagement—clicks, likes, comments, and shares—that content receives." And since people are 3 times more likely to trust the information coming from an employee than that from a CEO, encouraging employees to share information from your company page will increase your reach exponentially.

Companies who participated in the pilot of Elevate noticed 6 times more sharing engagement by employees, likely due to the ease in sharing via handheld devices with anyone in their social media networks. So utilize this feature to empower your employees to be "social professionals." Of course, make sure they're up to speed on your rules for posting.

Also, be sure to check your company page analytics regularly to see how you're doing! LinkedIn® Elevate features its own set of micro-conversion level analytics as well.

For more information on setting up and leveraging company pages, see LinkedIn's Company Pages FAQ.[3]

Results to Expect

Your company will present a professional and savvy image on LinkedIn. The company will be searchable on LinkedIn not only in multiple ways: through your profile and the profiles of your employees, and also through Company Pages. This multiple exposure will boost your company in LinkedIn's search rankings *as well as on Google*.

Good news: LinkedIn currently has the highest lead conversion rate of any social media platform. According to one study, 5000+ businesses reported that LinkedIn enjoyed an average 2.74% visitor to conversion ratio, as opposed to 0.69% for Twitter and 0.77% for Facebook. Another study showed that LinkedIn was responsible for landing 64% of social referrals on business home pages. Facebook and Twitter were far less effective at 17% and 14% respectively.

More traffic to your website means more sales. Don't miss out on this opportunity for FREE marketing and

---

2 10 Things B2B Marketers Should Be Doing on LinkedIn - http://tinyurl.com/modavg2

3 LinkedIn's Company FAQ - http://tinyurl.com/pr78xc7

Search Engine Optimization!

For the metrics-minded, you'll be happy to know that LinkedIn provides analytics for your page's activities!

To view them, from your profile page hover over your avatar in the upper right and select Company Page from the drop down menu.

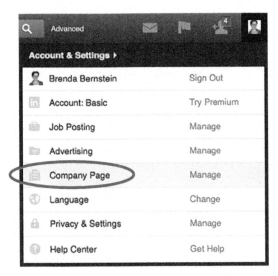

From your company page, click on Analytics just below the company name:

You'll be able to review these analytics:

- Statistics on all of the updates you've posted, including impressions (or reach) and percent engagement.
- Demographics and trends of your followers, including how you compare with similar companies.
- Visitor statistics and demographics.

Here's a sample from the beginning of March 2015:

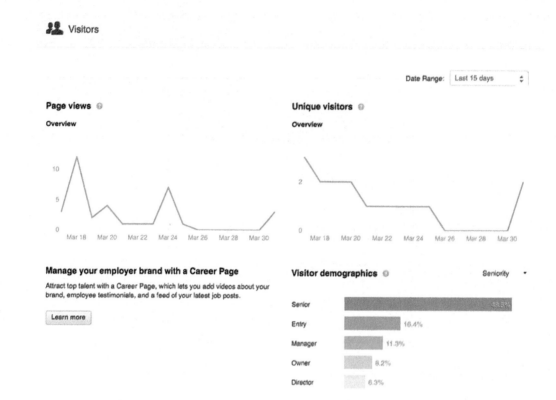

Use these statistics to identify your target audience and measure what activity has generated the most views of your page. Then do more of what's working to build your audience and client base!

BONUS TIP #3

Create a Profile Badge

The Problem

If an employer or client receives your resume or an email from you and wants to look at your LinkedIn profile, you want to make it easy for them to do so.

The Tune-Up

To create an email signature that links to your LinkedIn profile page, visit https://www.linkedin.com/profile/profile-badges.

To create a button on your resume or any other document that links to your LinkedIn profile, read LinkedIn's instructions for adding a profile badge to your blog, online resume or website. If you simply want to link one of the images on this page to your LinkedIn Profile, first copy and paste the badge that you like into your document (you might want to use your snipping tool) . . . here are some choices:

If you are using MS Word, click on the newly pasted-in badge image, then go to the Insert menu and click on Hyperlink.

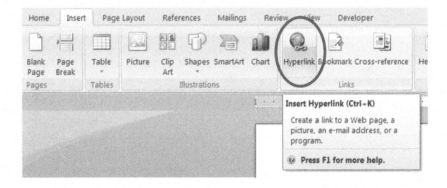

Then copy and paste your LinkedIn URL into the Address field:

Hit OK and your image will be linked to your LinkedIn profile.

Results to Expect

Recruiters, employers and clients will have everything they need at their fingertips to get a full picture of who you are and what you offer. They will be ready, if they like what they see, to invite you to take the next step, whether that is submitting a cover letter or scheduling an interview or a meeting. Of course this means you have your work cut out for you to present outstanding materials in all the places your target audience might be looking!

BONUS TIP #4

For Unemployed Job Seekers:
What to Put in Your Headline, Activity Updates
and Experience Sections

Some of the most common questions I receive from job seekers are "What should I put in my headline?" "Should I put 'Seeking New Opportunities' in my Activity Updates?" "What should I put in my current Experience section if I'm not currently working?"

The Problem

We all know that despite the clear fact that unemployment does not equate with lack of talent or skill, many employers prefer to hire people who are currently employed. Ultimately, there will often be no perfect way to hide the fact that you are not currently working. However, there are many choices of how to approach this situation in your LinkedIn profile.

The Tune-Up

The biggest problem with figuring out how to handle unemployment is that there is no one right answer! What follows are some of my thoughts on how to approach each of the three sections (Headline, Status Bar and Experience) as an unemployed job seeker.

Headline: Stock your headline with keywords relevant to your industry (see the very first section in this book!) The most important thing you can do to appear in searches (in conjunction with expanding your network) is to have the right keywords in your profile. Whenever possible, also make your headline compelling with a unique selling proposition in order to increase interest once people find you (See Mistake #1). These are the most important factors in getting attention from recruiters and hiring managers.

If you have additional characters available, you can try out putting "Seeking Opportunities" or "Open to New Opportunities" in your headline. Some recruiters search for the word "Opportunities" and approach people they know are looking for a job. Others will, as a rule, never contact anyone with "Seeking New Opportunities" in their headline. If you choose this route, therefore, change things up every month or so and see what kind of attention you're getting. Do what works best for you.

Activity Updates: I do not recommend posting anything about seeking opportunities in your activity updates. Instead, use this feature to write about what you're learning, what's inspiring you, and the success you're having in your life! Did you just get a new certification? An interview offer? Why not report that to the world? News like that will likely make you attractive to another organization. For more on how to post Activity Updates, see Mistake #12.

Current Experience: Unemployed job seekers may approach this section in several ways. Following are some of the most common. Note that before changing your current job title, you should turn off your Activity Updates in your Privacy Settings. Wait at least a day before and after turning these notifications off and back on, as the change does not always take effect immediately. Also, be aware that when you change your current job title, LinkedIn will ask if this is your current title. Say "NO" to avoid having your headline replaced by the new title. You will be tempted to click "YES" but don't do it! This way your headline will remain the way you wrote it, with all the keywords you worked so hard to put in there (also see Mistake #1).

Here are some options for how to populate your current job title when you are not employed full time:

1. **"Consultant."** Some job seekers will create an Experience section that makes it look like they are a consultant. *Only do this if you are truly doing consulting work and can say something about it!* Otherwise it will look like you are hiding something.

2. **"Manager, LinkedIn Group."** I generally do not recommend listing management of a LinkedIn group as a current job title. For most people, this position is nowhere near a full- time job. An exception to this guideline would be if you have built an e-group empire that is growing by leaps and bounds, with hundreds of thousands of members, and that is turning into a revenue-generating machine!

3. **"Job Title at Seeking Opportunities."** As I suggested in the Headline section of this tip, some recruiters might respond positively to this current experience description and others might not. You can try different things to see what works best for you.

4. **Volunteer.** If you are participating significantly as a volunteer and have major accomplishments to report, putting a volunteer role in the current experience section may be appropriate. Otherwise, use the Volunteer Experience and Causes section to report your volunteer participation. According to Link Humans, "42% of hiring managers surveyed by LinkedIn said they view volunteer experience as equivalent to formal work experience"!

5. **Part-Time.** If you are employed part-time, there is absolutely no requirement that you reveal that fact. Complete the section as if the position were a full-time job. Enter the company name, your job title and accomplishments, and leave it at that.

6. **Parent.** If you are a stay-at-home mom or dad, you can list "Stay-at-Home Parent" as a job title; but if you were engaged in projects during that time, list those instead, with appropriate titles and descriptions.

7. **Blank.** This strategy is recommended by many recruiters. Their philosophy is that if you're not employed, honesty is the best policy.

You'll probably need to experiment a bit here. Different strategies work better for different people. The great thing about an online profile is that you can change it whenever you want and find out what works best for you. Just remember to take control of your privacy settings when you make any changes.

Results to Expect

I wish I could tell you what strategy will get you the biggest response if you are an unemployed job seeker. The fact is, some recruiters and hiring managers prefer to see "Seeking New Opportunities" and others prefer to see a position title or no current position at all. Experiment until you get the results you want!

BONUS TIP #5

Don't Violate LinkedIn's Terms of Service

LinkedIn's User Agreement is located at https://www.linkedin.com/legal/user-agreement.

The Problem

This document contains many rules and regulations that you might not be aware of, and that, if violated, could cause your account to be suspended or terminated. The section entitled "DO's and DON'Ts" is especially important to read. You might discover that you are violating one or more of the items on this list. You might also discover that another member is violating the user agreement.

Did you know that it is a violation of LinkedIn's User Agreement to "[i]nvite people you do not know to join your network"? The definition of "know" is not clear, and I have never heard of LinkedIn's enforcing this one.

Members are also not allowed to use workarounds for including contact information or keywords, such as putting a telephone number or other personal identification information in a field where there is no official field provided by LinkedIn for that purpose.

Do you think spammers are using bots to download your contact information or send you unsolicited messages? If they are doing so, they are violating the user agreement.

LinkedIn does have some measures in place to prevent damage to your account besides disallowing such behavior in its user agreement. To deter people from hacking into your account, LinkedIn will block the IP of anyone who tries to log in from an IP address it does not recognize. If this happens, you will receive the following notice:

Hi Brenda,   Linked in.

Someone just tried to sign in to your LinkedIn account from an unfamiliar location (United States), so we want to make sure it's really you.

If you did try to sign in:
Please use this verification code to complete your sign in: 663318

If you did NOT try to sign in:
1. Type www.linkedin.com/settings directly into your browser.
2. Sign in with your email address and password.
3. Next to the Password field in the upper left corner, click the "Change" link to change your password.

Thanks for helping us keep your account secure,
The LinkedIn Team

Blocked login attempt from 66.252.67.202 (United States)

When you log into your account consistently from a location other than your primary IP address, you might receive a notice asking if you would like to change the location on your profile:

The Tune-Up

First of all, read LinkedIn's User Agreement! It's essential to be aware of all the terms of service that apply to you.

Do not include phone numbers or email addresses in your Headline. Do not include keywords in your Name field. Follow the rules!

Safeguard your login information so that no other parties can access your account. You can see all of the places you're currently logged in by going to Privacy & Settings and from the top section of the page, clicking on See where you're logged in under Your active sessions.

If you receive a notice that someone tried to hack into your profile, change your password immediately!

If you experience any violations of LinkedIn's User Agreement or have questions about its terms, contact LinkedIn. Here's how:

Contact them online:
https://help.linkedin.com/app/ask/path/uaq/

Or by physical mail. For Members in the United States:

LinkedIn Corporation
Attn: User Agreement Issues 2029 Stierlin Court Mountain View, CA 94043

For Members outside the United States: LinkedIn Ireland
Attn: User Agreement Issues
Gardner House, Wilton Place, Wilton Plaza Dublin 2 94043
Ireland

Results to Expect

You'll retain your LinkedIn membership status so you can create relationships and produce results through LinkedIn for many years to come.

BONUS TIP #6

Take Control Over Your Appearance!

The Problem

You might not like the order in which your profile sections appear. Did you know that you can rearrange them?

The Tune-Up

In Edit mode, just scroll over the up and down arrow by the title of any section and you can move it to the position of your choice! You will see a pop-up message that says "Drag to rearrange profile sections." You can put your sections in any order you choose. The only exception is the Activity section, which is immovable.

Summary

Drag to rearrange profile sections

► Do you struggle with writing about yourself? Stop trying to do it alone!

We work intensively and personally with job seekers, college/MBA applicants and companies to create powerfully written resumes, application essays, LinkedIn profiles and marketing content.

Another trick is to put a note in your Summary about anything important in your profile that might otherwise go unnoticed. For instance, when I had a video testimonial as part of my profile, my summary stated:

★ Scroll down to see the SlideShare presentation that goes along with the lovely music you're hearing!

You might want to insert a similar note about recommendations you have attached, presentations you have inserted, or anything else to which you want to draw attention.

Results to Expect

Taking control of the appearance of your LinkedIn profile will ensure that the most important sections are also the most prominent. No longer will important information be lost in a sea of LinkedIn sections! You can direct your viewers to view the parts of your KILLER profile that YOU want them to see.

BONUS TIP #7

Creating a Secondary Language Profile

As of February 2015, 70% of LinkedIn members are located outside of the US. Because such a large portion of users are multilingual and interested in connecting with people both inside and outside of English-speaking countries, I am including this special section on how to set up additional LinkedIn profiles that cater to secondary languages.

Note that the inspiration for this section came from one of my readers . . . so please do contribute your ideas if you have them!

LinkedIn supports the following languages:

English	Danish	Italian	Polish	Swedish
Arabic	Dutch	Japanese	Portuguese	Tagalog
Chinese (Simplified)	French	Korean	Romanian	Thai
Chinese (Traditional)	German	Malay	Russian	Turkish
Czech	Indonesian	Norwegian	Spanish	

Want more information? View a list of languages supported by LinkedIn mobile applications, visit: http://help. linkedin.com/app/answers/detail/a_id/999.

NOTE: You cannot change the default language of your profile once you've set it up in a particular language. It's recommended that you set up a secondary language profile instead.

Creating a Profile in Another Language

To create a profile in another language, go to your Profile page and click the down arrow to the right of your View profile as **button. Select** Create profile in another language:

Choose your language from the dropdown menu:

Edit Profile　　View Profile

Create Your Profile in Another Language

Language: Choose... ▾

Tip: If your language is not listed, select "Other"

First Name: Brenda

Last Name: Bernstein

Former/Maiden Name: 🔒

Professional "Headline":

▿ Essay & Resume Writer ★ Executive Resumes ★ Personal Statements ★ LinkedIn Profiles ★ Web Copy

Examples: Experienced Transportation Executive, Web Designer and Information Architect, Visionary Entrepreneur and Investor

[Create Profile] or Go back to Edit My Profile

You'll also want to update your Professional Headline. Then click Create Profile.

The language you select will determine the default language for your profile display and also the language in which you will receive messages from the LinkedIn Corporation. Content and messages will always be displayed in the language in which they are written. LinkedIn does not translate content or messages for you, so you will need to go through each section and update all necessary fields. Remember to save each section before continuing onto the next.

When a member signs in to LinkedIn and views your profile, they will see it in the language you chose when you set up your account; or, if you have multiple profiles in several languages, viewers will see the one most relevant to them. The viewer has the ability to choose from your language profiles by selecting one from the dropdown menu underneath your profile header.

🌐 View this profile in another language ▾

✓ **English**

Japanese

Chinese (Simplified)

Chinese (Traditional)

All of your language profiles will show up in search engines and have their own URL.

You can also delete a secondary language profile by selecting the language from this drop down list. Just select Delete this profile link and click Delete.

LinkedIn Profile Completion Checklist

Use this checklist to assess and update your LinkedIn profile based on the tips and strategies in this book.

_____ My profile uses highly searched keywords and an informative headline.

_____ My photo is a professional, closely cropped "head shot."

_____ My profile is 100% complete.

_____ Websites listed in my profile have clear, specific labels.

_____ I have a custom URL for my public profile (possibly with keywords included) .

_____ I have at least 500 connections.

_____ My profile contains a compelling summary section.

_____ My job duties and accomplishments are described in clear, concrete language.

_____ My profile is formatted consistently and is free of spelling, grammar, and punctuation errors.

_____ My profile is formatted attractively.

_____ I have completed the Skills section and chosen my top

_____ My profile is set to sharing my LinkedIn Activity Updates and other valuable information (do this after you finish making your updates).

_____ I have taken advantage of Special Sections to provide additional detail about my accomplishments.

_____ I have attached Portfolio items in my Summary and Experience Sections.

_____ I have used the Jobs function on LinkedIn (if you are a job seeker or employer).

_____ I am a member of at least seven LinkedIn groups and participate regularly in group discussions.

_____ I have at least three (and preferably 10), well-written recommendations.

_____ I review my LinkedIn profile at least monthly, and update it when needed.

_____ I have exported and saved a backup copy of my profile in .pdf format.

_____ If I own a businesses, I have created a Company page.

_____ I have a Profile Badge and I use it in my email signature.

_____ If I am unemployed, my Headline, Activity Updates and Experience sections contain appropriate information.

_____ I am in full compliance with LinkedIn's Terms of Service.

_____ I have taken over control of my profile's appearance by putting the sections in the order I prefer.

_____ If I am bilingual, I have created a Secondary Language Profile.

_____ **Total Completed**

Notes:

_____

_____

_____

_____

_____

_____

_____

_____

_____

_____

_____

_____

_____

APPENDIX B

Character Limits for your LinkedIn Profile Sections

When writing your LinkedIn profile sections, it is helpful to know the character limits you are working with! Here are some of the most important ones to help you plan your work and work your plan on LinkedIn:

Character Limits

First name: 20 characters

Last name: 40 characters

Maiden name: 40 characters **URL:** 5-30 characters

Professional Headline: 120 characters

Website Anchor Text: 30 characters

Website URL: 256 characters

Address: 1,000 characters (visible only 1st degree connections)

Activity update: 700 characters (only 140 will transfer to Twitter)

Long-Form Posts: No limit

Summary: 2,000 characters

Specialties: 500 characters

Company Name: 100 characters

Job Title (in Experience section): 100 characters

Education/Degree: 100 characters

Description (in Experience section): 2,000 characters

Activities and Societies (in Education): 500 characters

Education Description: 1,000 characters

Additional Info/Interests: 1,000 characters

Honors & Awards: 1,000 characters

Skills: 61 characters each (up to 50 skills)

Personal Info-Instant messenger: 25 characters

Other Limits

Number of direct, first-level connections: 30,000

Number of outbound invitations: 3,000 (you can request more, 100 at a time)

Maximum number of groups: 50

Maximum groups managed by one individual: 10

Maximum groups moderated by one individual: 50

Number of private messages you can send to any of your group members per month: 15[1]

(For more group-related limits, read General Limits for LinkedIn Groups.[2]

---

1 Communicating with a Fellow Group Member - http://tinyurl.com/nm5z2l3

2 General Limits for LinkedIn Groups - https://help.linkedin.com/app/answers/detail/a_id/190

APPENDIX C

LinkedIn Image Dimensions

All LinkedIn images can be uploaded in PNG, JPEG/JPG or GIF formats.

Profile Photo

Max size 4 MB. Image must be between 200 x 200 and 500 x 500. If either width or height exceeds 4000 pixels, your photo will not upload.

Company Pages

Banner Image: Max size 2 MB. Image must be 646 x 220 pixels or larger. Standard Logo: Max size 2 MB. Image will be resized to fit 100x60 pixels Square Logo: Max size 2 MB. Image will be resized to fit 50x50 pixels

Showcase Pages

Banner Image: Max size 2 MB. Image must be 974 x 330 pixels or larger.

LinkedIn Premium

Background Photo: Max size 4MB. Image must be between 1000 x 425 and 4000 x 4000 pixels. Profile Photo: Max size 4 MB. Image must be between 450 x 450 and 4000 x 4000 pixels.

Career Pages

Cover Image: 974 x 238 pixels.

(Career Pages are a paid feature. To learn more, read LinkedIn Career Pages—Overview.[1]

1 LinkedIn Career Pages - Overview - http://tinyurl.com/p6uu4e9

APPENDIX D

LinkedIn's 25 Hottest Skills & Overused Buzzwords

LinkedIn's 25 Hottest Skills

In 2013, LinkedIn began publishing the 25 "hottest" skills that get people hired. Since then, LinkedIn has worked to improve their algorithms in order to provide you with the most accurate representation of the skills that are trending. If you have this year's skills, you may have been on the radar of several hiring companies.

Below is LinkedIn's 2014 list. Depicted here are what LinkedIn deems the most sought-after skills by recruiters all over the world. If you're interested in a breakdown of this list by the following countries, see the LinkedIn Blog original article, The 25 Hottest Skills That Got People Hired in 2014.[1]

Australia	Brazil	Canada	France
India	Netherlands	South Africa	United Arab Emirates
United Kingdom	United States		

In a computer and nanotech-driven world, it's no surprise that the hottest skills right now are in the STEM (Science, Technology, Engineering and Math) category, followed closely by Data Analysis.

The 25 Hottest Skills of 2014 on LinkedIn

1	Statistical Analysis and Data Mining	14	User Interface Design
2	Middleware and Integration Software	15	Recruiting
3	Storage Systems and Management	16	Digital and Online Marketing
4	Network and Information Security	17	Computer Graphics and Animation
5	SEO/SEM Marketing	18	Economics
6	Business Intelligence	19	Java Development
7	Mobile Development	20	Channel Marketing
8	Web Architecture and Development Framework	21	SAP ERP Systems
9	Algorithm Design	22	Integrated Circuit (IC) Design
10	Perl/Python/Ruby	23	Shell Scripting Languages
11	Data Engineering and Data Warehousing	24	Game Development
12	Marketing Campaign Management	25	Virtualization
13	Mac, Linus and Unix Systems		

---

1 The 25 Hottest Skills That Got People Hired in 2013 - http://tinyurl.com/mnv4vdo

Do you need to add some of these skill sets to your LinkedIn profile? See Mistake #11 for tips on adding Skills to your profile.

LinkedIn's Overused Buzzwords

LinkedIn also intermittently provides a list of overused professional buzzwords for the year. Here's the list from 2014, as published in LinkedIn's Official Blog article, Brand YOU Year: How to Brand Yourself Without Sounding Like Everyone Else.[2] For my blog discussing this year's list, see Overused LinkedIn Buzzwords of 2014 . . . At Long Last!! [3]

> The Top 10 Overused Buzzwords in LinkedIn Profiles are as follows:
> 1. Motivated (resurrected to #1 after dropping off the list in 2013)[4]
> 2. Passionate (making its debut as a buzzword!)
> 3. Creative (holding strong at #3)
> 4. Driven (up from #8 in 2013)
> 5. Extensive Experience (absent from 2013's list, this one was #1 in 2010!)
> 6. Responsible (dropped from #1 in 2013)
> 7. Strategic (dropped from #2 in 2013)
> 8. Track Record (back on the list after its last appearance as #6 in 2012)
> 9. Organizational (slowly dropping: #2 in 2012; #7 in 2013)
> 10. Expert (dropped from #6 in 2013)

Words like innovative and analytical have disappeared from the list this year, but if buzzword history shows us anything, they will be back! What would it take for you to scrub your LinkedIn profile clean of overused and overrated buzzwords? Sometimes you really do need to be "creative" to succeed in presenting yourself in a unique way.

---

2 Top 10 Overused LinkedIn Profile Buzzwords of 2013 - http://blog.linkedin.com/2013/12/11/buzzwords-2013/

3 Overused LinkedIn Buzzwords of 2014 . . . At Long Last!! - http://theessayexpert.com/blog/overused-linkedin-buzzwords-of-2014/

4 Top 10 Overused LinkedIn Profile Buzzwords of 2013 - http://blog.linkedin.com/2013/12/11/buzzwords-2013/

APPENDIX E

Information on Paid Accounts

A survey by Wayne Breitbarth[1] found that 84.4% of LinkedIn users use the free account; only 15.1% of those surveyed paid to use LinkedIn.

I would be willing to guess that most of the paid subscribers are recruiters.

Nevertheless, for some people, features like being able to send InMail, viewing more information about who viewed your profile, and having more organizational capabilities is worth the price of the subscription.

LinkedIn frequently offers free month-long trials, which you might want to take advantage of. For more information, go to LinkedIn Free and Upgraded Premium Accounts.[2]

---

1 Portrait of a LinkedIn User - http://www.powerformula.net/linkedin-infographic/

2 LinkedIn Free and Upgraded Premium Accounts - https://help.linkedin.com/app/answers/detail/a_id/71

APPENDIX F

LinkedIn Help

Need LinkedIn Technical Help?

From time to time, you might encounter technical questions about how LinkedIn works, or LinkedIn might change something unexpectedly. For those sticky situations, I recommend contacting LinkedIn Help.

There is also a public forum for LinkedIn-related help topics. You can access the forum at http://community. linkedin.com/questions/ask.html

LinkedIn offers these discussion tips for posting in the help forum:
1. Forum discussions are public. Please don't write anything you don't want the world to see, such as passwords, phone numbers, and email addresses.

2. Before you post, search for similar existing discussions that might help.

3. Include any details that will help others respond to your question.

4. Add tags that will help other members find your discussion.

Free Webinar and Podcast Recordings

I've hosted multiple webinars and made guest appearances on several radio shows on the topic of LinkedIn, job search, resume writing and more. See The Essay Expert's Webinars & Podcasts Page[1] for recordings and upcoming events.

Free Bi-Weekly LinkedIn Tips Right in Your Inbox

Subscribe to The Essay Expert's LinkedIn and Professional Writing e-list[2] to receive helpful emails that include news, tips and tricks on how to best utilize LinkedIn.

---

1 The Essay Expert Webinars & Podcasts - http://theessayexpert.com/webinars-podcasts/

2 The Essay Expert's LinkedIn and Professional Writing e-list - http://theessayexpert.com/subscribe-to-the-weekly-blog/

APPENDIX G

Important Opportunities to Give and Receive

Get Free Lifetime Updates

LinkedIn is constantly changing, and I publish new versions of the PDF version of this book approximately three times per year. As a reader of the print book, you can get lifetime updates of the PDF book when I issue a new edition.

Sign up to receive free lifetime updates at http://theessayexpert.com/killer-e-book-updates/. We'll email you a link to a fresh copy every time a new edition of the e-book is published. What a great deal!

We Want Your Feedback!

We hope you've enjoyed *How to Write a KILLER LinkedIn Profile*! Did you find this book helpful? Please share a review on Amazon[1] and let others know about the value you received.

Want to see the answer to your LinkedIn question featured in the next edition of this book?

If you have a question regarding LinkedIn that you would like to see covered in the next edition, please email TEESupport@TheEssayExpert.com with your suggestion. The answer to your question might be featured in the next edition of *How to Write a KILLER LinkedIn Profile*.

Check Out Our Services

If you are still stuck on how to write your LinkedIn profile or your resume, consider The Essay Expert's LinkedIn[2] or Resume Writing services.[3] Contact us at TEESupport@TheEssayExpert.com or through our web form (http://theessayexpert.com/contact-us/), or call us at 608-467-0067. We look forward to working with you.

P.S. Book purchasers receive special discounts on LinkedIn services from The Essay Expert. See Appendix I for coupon codes you can use right now.

Get on My Lists

Want news and updates from The Essay Expert? Sign up for my Weekly Blog (http://theessayexpert.com/subscribe-to-the-weekly-blog/). You will receive a free e-book preview that you can give to a friend!

---

1 How to Write a KILLER LinkedIn Profile on Amazon - http://tinyurl.com/pzmcyvs

2 The Essay Expert's LinkedIn Profile Writing Services - http://theessayexpert.com/services-rates/linkedin-profiles/

3 The Essay Expert's Resume Writing Services - http://tinyurl.com/mwmanjm

Connect with The Essay Expert on Facebook

"Like" our Facebook Fan page (https://www.facebook.com/linkedinprofiletips) to connect with other readers and additional resources.

And of course, please Connect with me on LinkedIn (http://www.linkedin.com/in/brendabernstein)!

Thank you!
Here's to your success as you craft a
KILLER LinkedIn Profile!

APPENDIX H

Affiliate Program

Do you want to help out your friends and clients, and make money too? Register for The Essay Expert Affiliate Program[1] and earn 50% on every sale!

You probably have friends, clients and connections who are not getting the results they want from their LinkedIn profiles. If so, you might want to become an Essay Expert affiliate.

How to Write a KILLER LinkedIn Profile has been a top 10 best-seller in Amazon's Business Writing category since July 2012. It offers 18 detailed, easy-to-follow tips to improve your LinkedIn profile—PLUS 7 bonus tips!

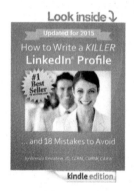

Look inside ↓

How to Write a KILLER LinkedIn Profile... And 18 Mistakes to Avoid: 2015 Edition (11th Edition) [Kindle Edition]

Brenda Bernstein ☑ (Author)

⭐⭐⭐⭐☆ ☑ (262 customer reviews)

Kindle Price: $9.97

- Length: 269 pages (estimated) ☑
- Word Wise: Enabled ☑
- Due to its large file size, this book may take longer to download
- Don't have a Kindle? Get your Kindle here.

The book is available as a downloadable .pdf on my site. When you partner with The Essay Expert through our affiliate program, you'll receive a 50% commission on every .pdf book sale.

I hope you'll take advantage of this opportunity not only to invite passive revenue to your current income stream, but also to provide your connections with the gift of a KILLER LinkedIn profile.

Registration is simple. Sign up and earn 50%: http://theessayexpert.com/affiliate-sign-up/

Thank you in advance for your support. And please let me know how I can help you!

---

1 The Essay Expert Affiliate Program - http://tinyurl.com/pyadju7

Discounted LinkedIn Services from The Essay Expert

If you're still struggling with what to write about yourself, it's time to stop!

You might wish to work with The Essay Expert directly. If so, we have discounts available for you on our LinkedIn packages. To take advantage of these offers, go to our LinkedIn Profile Writing page[1], order one of the following packages, and enter the coupon code.

LINKEDIN150 ($150 Discount)
- Executive LinkedIn Profile Complete

LINKEDIN100 ($100 Discount)
- LinkedIn Executive Summary Special Package
- Professional LinkedIn Profile Complete

LINKEDIN75 ($75 Discount)
- Professional LinkedIn Headline & Summary Special
- Professional LinkedIn Headline & Summary Only

LINKEDIN50 ($50 discount)
- 3 Hours – LinkedIn Profile Writing/Coaching

LINKEDIN40 ($40 discount)
- 2 Hours – LinkedIn Profile Writing/Coaching

LINKEDIN30 ($30 discount)
- 1 Hour – LinkedIn Profile Writing/Coaching
- Report + On-Demand Questions
- Report Only
- 45-Minute LinkedIn Coaching Session + On-Demand Question
- 45-Minute LinkedIn Coaching Session Only

---

1 The Essay Expert's LinkedIn Profile Writing Services - http://theessayexpert.com/services-rates/linkedin-profiles/

Here's what people are saying about The Essay Expert's LinkedIn Services:

"Compliments to Brenda and her team for delivering a product that exceeded my expectations. The whole transaction from order to acknowledgment, scheduling and follow through, was delivered as promised in a very personable and professional manner. Well worth the investment made."

— **Linda Batista**, PMP, Finance Manager, Dallas/Fort Worth Area

---

"Brenda did a fabulous job reviewing my LinkedIn profile. It was well worth the investment and I highly recommend her service. I received a detailed explanation and edits for each category, all the way down to recommendations. I feel much more confident in my LinkedIn profile after Brenda's review. Thanks for a job well done!"

— **William L. Mitchell**, IT Consultant, Greater New York City Area

---

"I found the response time to be very quick, the quality of work to be excellent, and the creativity of the suggestions to be superb. I believe the value I received from the review significantly exceeds the amount that I paid for the service. You must try it!"

— **Mike Robar**, Director of Mortgage Operations, Greater Philadelphia Area

---

"The engagement exceeded expectations -- from the immediate reply to me here in China, to on- time turnaround, to The Essay Expert's ability to understand my needs. Thank you very much. Highly recommended!

— **Roger McDonald**, Deputy Managing Director, Newport, UK

"The best investment I've made in my search efforts! Thank you!"

— **David McKnight**, President at Digital Publishing Innovation, Madison, WI

"As a result of my LinkedIn profile changes, I have had 17 requests made of me to meet with various potential clients and partners!"

— **Aaron W.**, Business Consultant, Madison, WI

"My new profile meets my goals of a 'Killer profile'—and the process was done quickly, concisely, professionally. Nice job."

— **Jim Masloski**, Customs Brokerage Professional, Sioux Falls, SD

APPENDIX J

LinkedIn For Students & LinkedIn Youniversity

The following Youniversity tools can be accessed via your Education tab:

LinkedIn for Students[1] is filled with videos and tips on the most effective ways to use LinkedIn, from building your personal brand to getting an internship.

- Available videos cover a variety of topics to get you started with networking, discovering your career passion, and prepping for interviews. You'll also find checklists and tip sheets for building your student profile and utilizing LinkedIn's Alumni tools.

- **Student Jobs 101** provides tips for optimizing your LinkedIn profile, approaching the college job hunt, and applying for internships and entry-level positions.

- **Jobs for Students and Recent Graduates** is LinkedIn's search engine for internship positions and jobs for recent graduates. Search by industry for a list of positions that may interest you.

- **LinkedIn for Students Articles** contains a collection of articles written by LinkedIn's top writers related to college and career.

LinkedIn Youniversity[2] is designed to help students find the perfect college. It's a one-stop hub where you can communicate with other students, advisors and future classmates.

1 LinkedIn for Students - https://university.linkedin.com/linkedin-for-students

2 LinkedIn Youniversity - https://www.linkedin.com/edu/

Here are just a few of its features:

- **University Rankings** - Find out which schools are best rated in terms of placing new graduates. Read how LinkedIn attains these ratings in LinkedIn's Official Blog article, Ranking Universities Based on Career Outcomes.[3]

- **University Finder** - Just tell LinkedIn what you want to do and they'll show you the top schools for that industry career.

- **Field of Study Explorer** - LinkedIn takes your field of study (based on your profile) and lists the top business and connections for you.

- **Decision Boards** - Create a pin board where you can keep all of your top picks from your University Rankings, Finder and Field of Study tools in one place, plus get start conversations to get advice from people you trust and respect.

  When you select a preferred university and/or field of study, your Decision Board will appear on your profile page. Visitors will then have the opportunity to help you make your decision based on their experiences.

Decision Board

Could you help me make some choices about my education?
I'm thinking about 2 universities.

View board

Background

For more information on how to use LinkedIn Youniversity, read LinkedIn's Official Blog article, Social + Data = Better Decisions for Students.[4]

Add to Profile

LinkedIn's Add to Profile feature will make adding your degrees and certification to your LinkedIn Profile a breeze. Released to colleges and universities in March 2015, "educational institutions can embed a simple link on their websites and in emails sent directly to graduates. When graduates click the Add-to-Profile button, they'll have the option to add that achievement directly to the 'Education' section of their LinkedIn profile by previewing it and hitting Save."

---

3 Ranking Universities Based on Career Outcomes - http://tinyurl.com/o2gg6ag

4 Social + Data = Better Decisions for Students - http://tinyurl.com/q9nft2y

For more information on this feature read the LinkedIn Blog article, LinkedIn Opens Up Profiles to Higher Education Partners with One-Click Program.[5]Institutions currently utilizing this feature include:

Arizona State University

Kaplan University

University of California, San Diego

Villanova University

George Washington University

Full Sail University

University of Manchester

University of Cambridge

Universitas Indonesia

The Open University

Algonquin College

Keio University

University of Melbourne

---

5 LinkedIn Opens Up Profiles to Higher Education Partners with One-Click Program
http://blog.linkedin.com/2015/03/18/add-to-profile/

APPENDIX K

PURCHASE BRENDA'S E-BOOKS

Go to our e-book page on Amazon at http://tinyurl.com/ou56bjf.

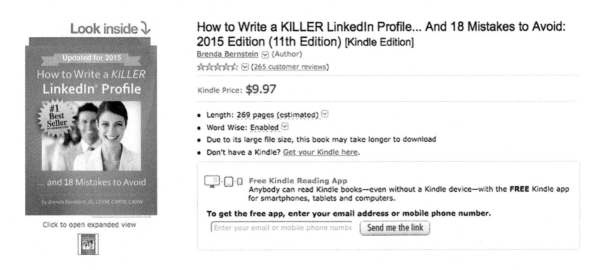

Are You a Job Seeker?

LinkedIn has still not eliminated the need for a static resume! To that end, I've written 2 resume do-it-yourself books. These are easy-to-read, practical and up-to-date guides that will take you through the resume writing process step by step, from thinking through your approach to creating a great format, crafting effective branding statements and bullets, and handling specific challenges. Available on Amazon:

How to Write a WINNING Resume . . . 50 Tips to Reach Your Job Search Target $6.97 US
(You can sign up to receive a free excerpt of this book at http://theessayexpert.com/subscribe-to-the-weekly-blog/.)

How to Write a STELLAR Executive Resume . . . 50 Tips to Reach Your Job Search Target $9.97 US
(You can sign up to receive a free excerpt of this book at http://theessayexpert.com/subscribe-to-the-weekly-blog/.) I've also partnered with Mary Elizabeth Bradford to offer a trusted and award-winning resource, ***The Job Search Success System***[1]. Your KILLER LinkedIn profile and WINNING resume will be greatly complimented by this 10-step system!

CPSIA information can be obtained
at www.ICGtesting.com
Printed in the USA
BVOW07s2013150117

473552BV00001B/1/P